# And God Said...
## Let There Be
# Laughter!

# And God Said...
# Let
# There Be
# Laughter!

## Humorous & Inspiring
## Stories, Quotes & Quips

**Mary Hollingsworth**

**Guideposts**
New York, New York

*And God Said . . . Let There Be Laughter!*

ISBN-13: 978-0-8249-4736-1

Published by Guideposts
16 East 34th Street
New York, New York 10016
www.guideposts.com

Distributed by Ideals Publications, a Guideposts company
2630 Elm Hill Pike, Suite 100
Nashville, Tennessee 37214

ACKNOWLEDGMENTS
Every attempt has been made to credit the sources of copyrighted material used in this book. If any such acknowledgment has been inadvertently omitted or miscredited, receipt of such information would be appreciated.

Produced in association with Mark Sweeney & Associates, Bonita Springs, Florida.

Scripture quotations marked (GNB) are taken from the *Good News Bible*, the Bible in Today's English Version. Copyright © American Bible Society, 1966, 1971, 1976.

Scripture quotations marked (MSG) are taken from *The Message*. Copyright © 1993, 1994, 1995, 1996, 2000, 2001, 2002 by Eugene H. Peterson.

Scripture quotations marked (NIV) are taken from *The Holy Bible, New International Version*. Copyright © 1973, 1978, 1984 International Bible Society. Used by permission of Zondervan Bible Publishers.

And God said-- Let there be laughter! : humorous and inspiring stories, quotes, and quips / edited by Mary Hollingsworth.
     p. cm.
  ISBN 978-0-8249-4736-1
  1. American wit and humor. 2. Christian life--Anecdotes. I. Hollingsworth, Mary, 1947-
  PN6165.A53 2008
  818′.540208--dc22

                              2007040512

Cover and interior design by Marisa Jackson

Printed and bound in the United States of America

10  9  8  7  6  5   4  3

With love,
in memory of my dad,
Clyde Shrode—
a devoted minister
who taught
God's people, especially me,
how to laugh.

# Contents

# Acknowledgments

After twenty-five years in Christian publishing, I am more aware than ever that a book is a team effort. With the care and expertise of each person who touches it as it travels through the many and various processes required to bring a work to the market, it becomes stronger, finer and more readable. This book has been expertly influenced by a wonderful team, to whom I owe my heartfelt thanks and appreciation.

To God, Who gave us this delightful opportunity, pulled the team together and guided us as we worked.

To Guideposts, Marilyn Moore, Jonathan Merkh and especially David Morris, who share the vision for the book and have encouraged us along the way. Thanks for your partnership and faith in our team.

To the entire editorial and production team, who have contributed to the development of this book: Patty Crowley, Vicki Graham, Rhonda Hogan, Sue Ann Jones, Laura Kendall, Mary Kay Knox, Kathryn Murray, Nancy Norris, Stephanie Terry and Barbara Tork.

To Charlotte Greeson, my best friend for many years, who puts up with me when I bury my head for weeks at a time in a project like this.

And to Jazz and Samson, my two little Shih Tzus and funny, faithful companions, who sit at (or *on*) my feet, bark when it's time to eat, remind me when it's time to stop and play, make me take time out for treats, and show me what unconditional love is all about. You make me laugh.

# Introduction

Well, I know God didn't really say, "Let there be laughter," but in my mind He should have! And I'm convinced from reading His Word that, whether He actually said it in so many words or not, He surely meant for laughter to be part of our lives. After all, wouldn't life be a drudgery without the diversity and release of healthy laughter? The Bible does say, "A cheerful heart is good medicine" (Proverbs 17:22 NIV), and a cheerful heart will, no doubt, lead to happy laughter.

My dad taught me how to laugh. He was a minister of the Gospel for more than sixty years, and he loved to punch up his Sunday sermons and daily life with jokes and funny stories. In fact, he was known as the local joke-teller, and at potluck dinners or other church meetings, the church members would often say, "Clyde, tell us some preacher stories." He would grin and say, "Well, I might know one or two stories you'd like." And he'd have them in stitches for an hour.

Even at family get-togethers, Dad was the center of attention with his teasing and jokes, which rubbed off on all of us. So life at home is an ongoing series of laughter outbreaks, tickling the kids and teasing each other. And while Dad is now gone (he lived to a rich ninety-three years—see, it works!), the laughter he taught us permeates our hearts and continues to cement us as a family.

Dad would have loved *And God Said . . . Let There Be Laughter!* He actually collected books like this. Our team has giggled and mined our way through mountains of material to find the perfect nuggets for you. As a result, I think you'll agree that these pages are a delightful collection of funny stories, anecdotes, cartoons, one-liners, top-ten lists, and other comical bits and pieces on a variety of everyday topics that will meet you right where you live. Those topics include humor related to life in general, parenting, church life, the medical field, small towns, friendship, aging and women.

Frankly, I can't imagine life without laughter. I'm sure I would just suffocate and die without the life-sustaining joy it gives. So tune up your tickle box and get ready for some good, clean, old-fashioned hilarity. I hope you'll find yourself laughing along with us as you read.

There is a time for everything . . .
a time to weep and
a time to laugh. . . .

ECCLESIASTES 3:1, 4 NIV

# 1

# You've Gotta Be Kidding!

*Life can be a real yawner—a regular ho-hum existence—unless you kick out of the traces and have a little fun. Fortunately, life is full of funny, absurd moments to provide events that make us laugh and say, "You've gotta be kidding!"*

## HELP IS ON THE WAY

Not too long ago I had "one of those days."

I was feeling pressure from a writing deadline.

I had company arriving in a couple days, and the toilet was clogged.

I went to the bank, and the trainee teller processing my deposit had to start over three times.

I swung by the supermarket to pick up a few things, and the lines were serpentine.

By the time I got home, I was frazzled and sweaty and in a hurry to get something on the table for dinner. Deciding on Campbell's Cream of Mushroom soup, I grabbed a can opener, cranked open the can, then remembered I had forgotten to buy milk at the store.

Nix the soup idea.

Setting the can aside, I went to plan B, which was left-over baked beans. I grabbed a Tupperware from the fridge, popped the seal, took a look and groaned. My husband isn't a picky eater, but even *he* won't eat baked beans that look like caterpillars.

Really frustrated now, I decided on a menu that prom-ised to be as foolproof as it is nutrition-free: hot dogs and potato chips. Retrieving a brand-new bag of chips from the cupboard, I grabbed the cellophane and gave a hearty pull.

The bag didn't open.

I tried again.

Nothing happened.

I took a breath, doubled my muscle, and gave the bag a hearty wrestle.

With a loud pop, the cellophane suddenly gave way, rip-ping wide from top to bottom. Chips flew sky-high. I was left holding the bag, and it was empty.

It was the final straw. I let out a bloodcurdling scream.

"I CAN'T TAKE IT ANYMORE!"

My husband heard my unorthodox cry for help. Within minutes he was standing at the doorway to the kitchen, where he surveyed the damage: an opened can of soup, melting groceries, moldy baked beans and one quivering wife standing ankle-deep in potato chips.

My husband did the most helpful thing he could think of

at the moment. He took a flying leap, landing flat-footed in the pile of chips. And then he began to stomp and dance and twirl, grinding those chips into my linoleum in the process!

I stared.

I fumed.

Pretty soon I was working to stifle a smile.

Eventually I had to laugh.

And finally I decided to join him. I, too, took a leap onto the chips. And then I danced.

Now I'll be the first to admit that my husband's response wasn't the one I was looking for. But the truth is, it was exactly what I needed. I didn't need a cleanup crew as much as I needed an attitude adjustment, and the laughter from that rather funky moment provided just that.

> I didn't need a cleanup crew as much as I needed an attitude adjustment. . . .

So now I have a question for you, and it's simply this:

Has God ever stomped on your chips?

I know that, in my life, there have been plenty of times when I've gotten myself into frustrating situations and I've cried out for help, all the while hoping God would show up with a celestial broom and clean up the mess I've made of things.

What often happens instead is that God dances on my chips, answering my prayer in a completely different manner than I had expected, but in the manner that is best for me.

I'll be honest with you: Sometimes I sulk. Sometimes I dance.

I'm working on doing more of the latter than the former.

I guess the older I get the more I realize that he really does know what he's doing. He loves me and I can trust him.

Even when the chips are down.

*Karen Scalf Linamen*


## THE GREAT BOATING EXCURSION

After we had been married about ten years, my husband decided we would get a boat and take up skiing and fishing. Sounded like a good idea at the time.

The first time we went out was to Lake Grapevine for a trial run. About a half-hour before dark, we headed back to the marina, and he asked me, "Do you want to get the truck and trailer down the ramp, or do you want to drive the boat up on the trailer?" I said I didn't know how to back up a trailer, and I'd rather drive the boat up.

He went after the truck while I idled the boat in the harbor. When he got the trailer positioned on the ramp, I steered the boat into position, lined it up squarely, gave it the gas, and headed for the V at the front of the trailer. Mind you, the only boat driving I had done was to pull a skier, and that's how I took off for that trailer. *R-r-r-r-rmp!* I went airborne right through that V and into the bed of the truck.

Now, a marina is always very noisy—lots of people yelling, laughing, revving engines, kids screaming, even dogs barking. But when I drove the boat into the truck, an immediate hush fell on the place. It reminded me of that old commercial that said, "When E. F. Hutton speaks . . . " *Dead* silence.

We repaired the boat and the truck and made another run at fun on the lake. We went to Lake Texoma next. When it was time to leave, my husband said, "This time, *I'll* drive the boat. You bring the truck around. It's a four-lane ramp, and nobody is there. Just back straight down the ramp."

So I took the truck and started to back down this four-lane ramp. I would go back five feet, and the trailer would go to the left. I'd pull up, back down five feet, and the trailer would go to the right. For forty-five minutes I went up, back, right, up, back, left, while my husband stood in the boat groaning and turning red—not from the sun either.

Finally, some man came walking by. He asked if I needed help. I got out of the truck and said, "Please back this truck down that ramp." He did.

We made the three-hour drive from Lake Texoma to home in silence . . . *heavy* silence. But we didn't give up. When we got home, the navigator told me that I would learn how to back a trailer . . . or else. The next day I was to practice in our driveway until I could do it. We had a circular driveway. I practiced entering from the left, and I practiced entering from the right. I practiced going down the straight of the driveway and around the circle. And I conquered. I did learn how to back up that trailer, and I was proud. *I'm ready now*, I thought.

So off we went to Lake Livingston for another fun adventure. It came time to leave. No sweat. I knew what to do. I'd practiced this. This ramp was only one lane. No problem. It was as wide as our driveway. I backed the truck and trailer down that ramp straight as an arrow. I grinned, feeling like a Cheshire cat, content and satisfied, until I heard him yelling, "Stop! STOP! STOP! Oh no! Why didn't you stop?"

Well, nobody had told me when to stop, and I was trying to get as close to the boat as I could. Now, I haven't tested all boat ramps, but that boat ramp had a big-drop off at the end of the concrete. (It was under water; so who knew?) I had backed so far that the trailer dropped off, still attached to the trailer hitch, but now hanging down in the water at a right angle to the truck.

Pulling the truck forward wouldn't lift the trailer. That just made it bang against the ramp. And six men couldn't lift it up against the water. So we had to call a maritime wrecker with a special winch that goes out into the water. After only a couple of hours we were out and on our way home . . . in silence, *dead* silence.

As we approached home, I timidly asked, "Do we want to continue having this much fun?" I really felt as if I'd had all the fun I could take. And I haven't been in a boat since.

*Anita Brock*

## YOU KNOW YOU'VE HAD A ROUGH DAY WHEN . . .

You drive into the repair shop, and your mechanic starts singing "I'm in the Money."

The deduction from the raise you just got is so big that you have to take a second job to replace the money you lost.

You tell the salesclerk you are looking for a pot holder and she directs you to the girdle department.

You are contemplating lining the rim of your boss's coffee cup with Super Glue.

You can't avoid the speeding ticket by flirting or crying because the police officer is a woman.

You eat an entire batch of brownies because you feel that "you deserve it."

After you drive home from work, you rip the "Have a Happy Day" bumper sticker off your car.

*You Know It's a Bad Day When . . .*

You turn on the morning TV news, and they're displaying emergency routes out of the city.

Your boss tells you not to bother taking off your coat.

The bird singing outside your window is a buzzard.

Your horn gets stuck when you're following a group of Hell's Angels on the freeway.

You put both contact lenses in the same eye.

Your pet rock snaps at you.

You call your answering service, and they tell you it's none of your business.

Your income-tax check bounces.

You wake up to discover your water bed has broken, and then you remember you don't have a water bed.

Your bar of Ivory soap sinks.

*Stan Jantz and Bruce Bickel*

## BLOOPERS

Classified ad:
"An unexpected vacancy for a
knife-thrower's assistant.
Rehearsals start immediately."

Newspaper ad:
"Extremely independent male.
Seventeen years old. Needs to rent room.
Call his mother at . . ."

Advertisement:
"Try our cough syrup.
You will never get any better."

For Sale:
Bulldog. Will eat anything.
Loves small children.

Child to mother after school:
"Our new teacher taught us all about fossils.
Before she came to class I didn't know
what a fossil looked like."

Child's definition of syntax:
"All the money collected at church from sinners."

Job seeker on application:
"I have an obsession for detail. I like to make sure
I cross my i's and dot my t's."

A small-town newspaper announcement:
"Gordie Jefferson celebrated his fifth birthday
with a party for eight little fiends."

Elderly lady to a friend:
"I will just die if nobody comes to my funeral."

"Ninety percent of the game is half mental."
(Yogi Berra on baseball, "the thinking man's game")

"I like long walks. Especially if they are taken by
people who annoy me."  (Fred Allen)

"I find television very educational. When it's on
I go into the other room and read a book."
(Groucho Marx)

*Phil Callaway*


## SITTING ON "PINS" AND NEEDLES

When you think about all the different numbers we
have to memorize throughout our lives, it's no wonder we're stressed.

It used to be we only had our Social Security, telephone,
and driver's license numbers to deal with. Nowadays, everything has a number. We've got credit card numbers, answering machine access codes, and personal identification
numbers (PINs) for everything from our checking account
to our video rental cards.

I didn't realize just how many different numbers had
been assigned to me until the other day when I called my
credit card's 800 number to inquire about my available
credit. From the moment that machine picked up the line, it
was a downhill journey for both of us.

"Welcome to our convenient automated credit line.
Please enter your account number."

I did that.

"For security purposes, and for your peace of mind,
please enter your PIN."

I did that too.

"Sorry, that is an incorrect PIN. Please try again."

I reentered my PIN.

"The PIN you entered does not match this account. If you would like to speak with an operator, please stay on the line. If you'd like another chance to reenter your PIN, you may do so at this time."

Okay, so maybe I was entering the wrong PIN. I decided to try another number that I had in my head.

"Sorry, that is an incorrect PIN."

Figuring I had inadvertently entered my savings account PIN, I tried another four digits.

"The PIN you entered does not match this account."

Well, maybe that was my telephone credit card PIN. I tried again.

I was wrong again.

"If you would like to speak with an operator," the voice repeated, "please stay on the line. If you'd like another chance to enter your PIN . . . and hopefully get it right this time . . . you may do so now."

I began  entering every number I knew—my Instant Teller PIN, my Social Security number, my driver's license number, my frequent flyer account numbers, my grocery store check cashing number and, finally, my address added to my age, number of children in my family and my grade point average in school, multiplied by my SAT score and divided by my systolic blood pressure (which happened to be steadily climbing at the moment).

"Sorry, but since you have failed to enter a correct PIN,"

the voice said, "we cannot grant you access to this account. Thank you for calling."

"No, wait!" I pleaded. "I *know* my PIN. I just need more time!"

I started pressing four-digit number combinations at random . . . 7734 . . . 9986 . . . 3395 . . . 2241 . . .

"You have exceeded the number of tries you are allowed," the recorded voice insisted.

"C'mon," I cried, continuing to press numbers as fast as I could. "I know my code. Give me another chance! Maybe it's 6948 . . . or 9375 . . . or maybe 3390."

"Please accept our apology for any inconvenience this may cause you . . ."

"4483. That's it! . . . Or how 'bout 2951? 9964? 5128?"

"It's been a pleasure serving you . . ."

"1148 . . . 9963 . . . 9024 . . ."

"Do have a nice day," it continued, as I frantically pressed more numbers, "and please know that all of this is for your own peace of mind. Good-bye."

"And so is this," I said as the machine disconnected me. And I cut up the card.

*Martha Bolton*


## EVERYTHING I NEED TO KNOW AS A WOMAN I LEARNED FROM LUCILLE BALL

I grew up watching the old black-and-white *I Love Lucy* show on television, laughing myself silly all the while. As

I became a woman, I was able to apply some of the lessons that I learned from Lucille Ball to daily life. Here are some things I learned:

Life is never really black-and-white.
You have to add the color.

Never, never, never tell your age.

Always keep your roots covered.

Reading directions is for wimps.

Never marry a foreigner.

If you can't speak the language, shout.

Never admit to anything.

Spaghetti isn't done if it won't stick to the ceiling.

Anytime you mess up, cry.

Anytime they're chasing you, cry.

Anytime you get caught, cry.

Don't worry, whatever it is, you can hide it in the closet.

To make something fit, diet, dye it, or dry it.

Beware of wax fruit, wax tulips, and wax noses.

Sticking to your budget shows no creativity.

Getting a job is easy; it's keeping it that's hard.

Grape juice won't wash off your feet.

Always keep a good scheme brewing.

Have a good disguise with you at all times.

When you meet important people, do something stupid to get their attention.

If you want to be a big success, sing off-key.

Never tango with eggs in your pocket.

And when all else fails, laugh, Honey, laugh.

*Mary Hollingsworth*

What is a *nanosecond*?

The time between when the light turns green and the guy behind you honks his horn!

*Marvin Phillips*

## THE THREE BEARS

It was a sunny morning in the big forest and the bear family was just waking up. Baby Bear went downstairs and sat in his small chair at the table. He looked into his small bowl. It was empty! "Who's been eating my porridge?" he squeaked.

Daddy Bear arrived at the table and sat in his big chair. He looked into his big bowl. It was also empty! "Who's been eating my porridge?" he roared.

Mummy Bear put her head through the serving hatch from the kitchen and yelled, "For Pete's sake, how many times do we have to go through this? It was Mummy Bear who got up first. It was Mummy Bear who woke everybody else in the house up. It was Mummy Bear who unloaded the dishwasher from last night and put everything away. It was Mummy Bear who went out into the cold early morning air to fetch the newspaper. It was Mummy Bear who set the table. It was Mummy Bear who put the cat out, cleaned the litter box and filled the cat's water and food dish. And now that you've decided to come downstairs and grace me with your presence . . . listen up, because I'm only going to say this one more time . . . I haven't made the porridge yet!

*Killy John and Alie Stibbe*

## HOW TO LIVE LONGER

The Japanese eat very little fat and suffer fewer heart attacks than the British or Americans.

The French eat a lot of fat and also suffer fewer heart attacks than the British or Americans.

The Japanese drink very little red wine and suffer fewer heart attacks than the British or Americans.

The Italians drink excessive amounts of red wine and suffer fewer heart attacks than the British or Americans.

The Germans drink a lot of beer and eat lots of sausages and fats and suffer fewer heart attacks than the British or Americans.

Conclusion: Eat and drink what you like. Speaking English is what kills you!

*J. John and Mark Stibbe*

Exhilaration is that feeling you get just after a great idea hits you and before you realize what's wrong with it.

*Michael Hodgin*

## STOPPED BY A COP

I went to high school in a small town in central Texas. Now, when I say small, I mean small. The sign outside of town said, "Home of 923 nice people and one old grouch."

There were only twenty-one seniors in my graduating class, and our favorite pastime was to sit downtown on the corner and watch the through traffic stop and go at the only stoplight in town. They might not have to stay in our little town, but we at least made them stop and look both ways before they went on to bigger and better places.

My best friend's dad in that small town was a funeral director. My dad was the minister of a small church in town, and he worked for the funeral director part-time. Like many funeral homes of old, this one was in a big, old house.

The family lived in one side, and the funeral home was operated out of the other side. Since there was no radio station in town, and the newspaper only came out once a week, the only way we knew someone was "lying in state" at the funeral home was if the front porch light was on. Then we had to call the funeral home and ask who it was, in case it was someone we knew. Since the funeral home was directly across the street from the post office, and there was no local mail delivery, everyone in town could see the front porch light every day when they went to get their mail. In short, it worked.

Several years after I graduated from high school, I was living in a large city about thirty miles from the small town. For a party I was having, and as a special joke for a friend's over-the-hill birthday, I borrowed an old, dilapidated child-size casket from my high-school friend's dad. I remembered it sitting in the storage area of the funeral home. We had used it a time or two to "bury our rivals" at pep rallies in high school.

It was a big hit at the party. The next evening, I put the little casket in the backseat of my car and drove down the freeway toward the small town to return it. About three miles outside of town, I was pulled over by a policeman, because I was speeding. When he came to the driver's window, I handed him my driver's license, a bit embarrassed by the incident.

"You're in a hurry, aren't you, ma'am?" he asked.

"Yes, I'm sorry, officer."

"Where are you going in such a hurry?"

Without thinking, I motioned toward the backseat and replied, "To the funeral home in town."

The patrolman casually shined his flashlight into the backseat to see what I was transporting. Then he quickly did a double take and a startled look came over his face as he realized he was looking at a child's casket.

"Oh. I . . . I . . . I see," he stumbled. "Well . . . follow me!"

And he turned and literally ran back through the darkness to his patrol car.

"Wait! Officer!" I called, suddenly realizing I had miscommunicated and wanting to tell him the truth. I even opened my door and started to go after him, but it was too late. He jumped into his car, flipped on his blinking lights and siren, and took off toward town, motioning for me to follow him. So, not knowing what else to do, I started my car and followed him into town.

When I arrived at the funeral home with a police escort, my friends at the funeral home were puzzled. Once again I tried to stop the policeman, but he just smiled sympathetically, waved, and drove away. And my friends became even more puzzled when I broke into gales of uncontrolled laughter.

*Mary Hollingsworth*


## THE LUMBERJACK

A slight, withered old man walked into the headquarters of a lumber company in Western Canada.

"I'd like a job as a lumberjack," he said.

The foreman politely tried to talk him out of the idea. After all, he was old, small and much too weak to fell trees.

Undaunted, the old man took up an ax and proceeded to chop down a huge tree in record time.

"That's just astounding," the foreman said.

"Where did you learn to fell trees like that?"

"Well," said the old man, "you've heard of the Sahara Forest?"

Replied the foreman, "You mean the Sahara Desert."

The old man said, "Sure, that's what it's called now."

*Executive Speechwriter Newsletter*

## QUICK THINKING

During World War II, a young man was asked to read an eye chart as part of his Army physical fitness examination.

"What chart?" asked the draftee.

The eye doctor replied, "Just sit down in that chair and I'll show you."

"What chair?" asked the draftee.

Well, that convinced the eye doctor and he deferred the young man because of poor eyesight. Released from serving in the army, the youth immediately celebrated his freedom by going to a movie. After the movie the lights came up and sitting in the seat next to the young man was the Army eye doctor.

"Excuse me," said the draftee, remaining calm, "Is this the bus to Duluth?"

*Executive Speechwriter Newsletter*

Walk a mile in his shoes before you criticize a man. Then, if he gets angry, you're a mile away and he's barefoot.

*Author unknown*

## UP IN THE AIR

A fellow named George owned an apartment complex and had just completed the exterior brickwork on the second floor. He had some bricks left over and was trying to decide the best way to get the load of bricks back down to ground level without breaking them. He noticed a fifty-five gallon barrel on the ground and thought, *I know what I'll do. I'll tie some rope around that barrel, hook a pulley to the second-floor eaves, and pull the barrel up to the second floor. Then I can load the bricks into the barrel and let it back down to the ground.*

So that's what he began to do. He tied the rope around the barrel, ran it over the pulley on the second floor, and pulled the barrel up to the second-story level. Then he tied the rope to the root of a nearby tree. He went up to the second floor balcony and loaded the bricks into the barrel. Then he went back downstairs, grabbed the rope and pulled it loose from the root.

Now, folks, that fifty-five gallon drum full of bricks was four times heavier than George. So the barrel shot down lickety-split, and George shot up lickety-split. And you know what happened. As George shot past the barrel, it hit his shoulder, slammed against his hip, and whomped his kneecap. The barrel crashed to the ground, and George's head smashed into the pulley above, cracking his skull. There he was, dangling by the rope from the second-story roof.

When the barrel hit the ground, the bricks were so heavy they knocked the bottom out of the barrel. So now George was heavier than the barrel. Yep! Down he went, and up it came. This time, the barrel caught him on the other side. It whomped his other knee, scraped past his other hip, broke his nose, and dumped him on top of the pile of leftover bricks below. He turned both ankles, scuffed up his shins, and the corners of the bricks punched him in the side. So George let out a yell and turned loose of the rope.

You guessed it. Now the barrel was four times heavier than the rope, so it came bombing down on top of George to finish the job from the previous hit-and-run. And George found himself lying in the hospital, bruised, sprained and broken, saying to himself, I don't know whether to file one insurance claim or five. . . .

I think most of us sometimes feel like George. Life has dumped us bruised, sprained and broken on its pile of left-overs. We're all whomped up and don't think we can even get up and walk away. That's just the nature of the way things happen in this life. Things do go wrong. Everything is always up in the air, at least here on earth!

*Paul Faulkner*

## FLYING

A photographer for a national magazine was assigned to take pictures of a raging forest fire. He was told that at the local airport a small plane would be waiting to take him up.

He got to the airstrip just before sundown, and sure enough, there was a small Cessna waiting. He jumped in with his equipment and shouted, "Let's go!" The man sitting in the pilot's seat swung the plane into the wind, and soon they were flying erratically through the air.

"Fly over the north side of the fire," said the photographer, "and make several low-level passes."

"Why?" asked the pilot.

"Because I'm going to take pictures!" yelled the photographer. "That's what photographers do!"

The pilot replied, "You mean—you're not the flight instructor . . . ?"

*J. John and Mark Stibbe*

Due to unforeseen circumstances, no clairvoyant meeting will be held tonight until further notice.

*Union-Sun and Journal*

## CRAFTY

I do crafts. No, wait, that's not quite right. I own crafts. Yes, that helps to bring into focus the blur of materials stuffed into assorted baskets, drawers, and boxes in my attic and basement.

My craft addiction has left partially done projects pleading for completion. I have snarls of thread once meant to be used in needlepoint and gnarly-looking yarn intended for an afghan. I have how-to books worn from my reading and rereading of the instructions. (I love reading; it's the doing that bogs me down.) Swatches of material, florist wire, paint brushes, grapevines and (every crafter's best friend) a glue gun—along with a myriad of additional stuff—greet me whenever I open my closet.

Every time I'm enticed into purchasing a new project, I think, *This one I'll do for sure.* I've attempted everything from oil painting, floral arranging, quilting and scherenschnitte (the German art of paper cutting) to quilling.

"Quilling?" you ask. For those of you unfamiliar with it, this craft requires you to wind itsy-bitsy, teeny-weeny strips of paper around the tip of a needle. Once they're wound, you glue the end, using a toothpick as an applicator so your paper coil doesn't spring loose. Then, with a pair of tweezers, you set your coil onto a pattern attached to a foam board, securing it with a straight pin. You are then ready to start the paper-twirling process over again. To be a good quiller, it helps if you, the crafter, are wound loosely.

I believe quillers (at least this one) have to be a few twirls short of a full coil to attempt this tedious art.

You may be wondering how many of those paper tidbits one needs to finish a piece. That depends on the size of your pattern. I chose a delicate, little snowflake. Taking into consideration that I'm a beginner (which is still true of every craft I've ever tried), I decided to select a small pattern and not overwhelm myself. (This would be like saying, "I think I'll go over Niagara in a barrel rather than a tub in hopes I won't get so wet.")

When I started my snowflake, I thought, *I'm going to make one of these for each of my friends and put them on the outside of their Christmas packages.* After five hours and a minuscule amount of noticeable progress, I reconsidered. *I will give these only to my best friends and include them in their gift boxes.*

A week later, I realized I didn't have a friend worth this kind of effort; only select family members would get these gems. And they would be all they'd get. I thought I would also include a contract for them to sign, agreeing to display their snowflakes well lit, under glass, in a heavy traffic area of their homes, all year.

Fifteen hours into my little winter-wonder project, I decided this would be the first and last paper wad I'd ever make . . . and I'd keep it for myself. It could be handed down in my family, generation after generation, in a time capsule, after my passing. I often wondered who the flake really was in this venture.

I suppose you're asking yourself, *Did she finish it?* Not yet, but I plan to (great inscription for tombstones).

I once attended a retreat where I was persuaded to join a wooden angel craft class. The angel done by the instructor (art major) as an example was adorable. Mine (craft minor) looked like an angel that might join a motorcycle gang.

Even that angel didn't get completed, because they ran out of heavenly parts. She had only one wing and was minus her halo. Actually, it was kind of sad. Today my fallen angel lies at the bottom of a box in my basement, covered with rotting quilt pieces and plastic ivy, still waiting for her ordination. May she rest in peace.

> We sell off and throw away our unfinished business, and then we go buy more.

I took a painting class for credit and received an A. Finally, something I could succeed in! Of course, if that was true, why didn't I have a picture to hang?

It hit me that I didn't have a painting anyone could identify, much less display. For one of our projects, we painted apples in a bowl. When I took it home, my friend thought it was a peacock.

I approached the instructor and asked how I had earned an A in her class. "For showing up every week," she responded. She must have the gift of mercy.

Les and I started hooking a two-foot-by-three-foot rug twenty-five years ago. We're almost to the halfway point.

We figure, in a joint effort, that we have hooked less than an inch a year and should complete it in the year 2012. You may want to get on our gift list.

I seem to be more into ownership than completion . . . and then I feel guilty. I've noticed I'm not alone in that. Some kindred spirits could stuff a landfill with their forsaken artistry. I wonder if that's why we have so many garage sales and so much garbage in this country. We sell off and throw away our unfinished business, and then we go buy more.

Words like *responsibility*, *follow through*, and *moderation* get lost in the shuffle as I push back one box of crafts to move in my newest project. Every time I haul out or hide away another abandoned endeavor, it reinforces a negative quality within me.

Besides, what happened to the notion "Waste not, want not"?

That's a great line. I wonder how it would look in cross-stitch?

Oops, there I go again.

*Patsy Clairmont*

I went to a bookstore and asked the woman behind the counter where the self-help section was. She said, "If I told you that would defeat the whole purpose."

*Brian Kiley*

## COMPLAINTS

Here are some actual maintenance complaints generally known as "squawks" or problems submitted recently by pilots to maintenance engineers. (P) is the problem logged by the pilot, and (S) marks the solution and action taken by maintenance engineers.

(P)     Target Radar hums

(S)     Reprogrammed Target Radar with the words

(P)     Test flight okay, except autoland very rough

(S)     Autoland not installed on this aircraft

(P)     Evidence of leak on right main landing gear

(S)     Evidence removed

(P)     DME volume unbelievably loud

(S)     Volume set to more believable level

(P)     Dead bugs on windshield

(S)     Live bugs on backorder

(P)     Friction locks cause throttle levers to stick

(S)     That's what they're there for

(P)     Number three engine missing

(S)     Engine found on right wing after brief search.

*J. John and Mark Stibbe*

## ACCIDENTALLY SPEAKING

The following is a series of twenty-one quotes taken from insurance or accident forms. They are the actual words of people who tried to summarize their encounters with trouble.

1. Coming home, I drove into the wrong house and collided with a tree I don't have.

2. The other car collided with mine without giving warning of its intentions.

3. I thought my window was down, but I found it was up when I put my hand through it.

4. I collided with a stationary vehicle coming the other way.

5. A van backed through my windscreen into my wife's face.

6. A pedestrian hit me and went under my car.

7. The guy was all over the road; I had to swerve a number of times before I hit him.

8. I pulled away from the side of the road, glanced at my mother-in-law, and headed over the embankment.

9. In my attempt to kill a fly, I drove into a telephone pole.

10. I had been shopping for plants all day and was on my way home. As I reached an intersection, a hedge sprang up obscuring my vision. I did not see the other car.

11. I had been driving for forty years when I fell asleep at the wheel and had an accident.

12. I was on the way to the doctor's with rear-end trouble when my universal joint gave way, causing me to have an accident.

13. To avoid hitting the bumper of the car in front, I struck the pedestrian.

14. As I approached the intersection, a stop sign suddenly appeared in a place where no stop sign had ever appeared before. I was unable to stop in time to avoid the accident.

15. My car was legally parked as it backed into the other vehicle.

16. An invisible car came out of nowhere, struck my vehicle, and vanished.

17. I told the police that I was not injured, but removing my hat, I found I had a skull fracture.

18. The pedestrian had no idea which direction to go, so I ran over him.

19. I was thrown from my car as it left the road. I was later found in a ditch by some stray cows.

20. The telephone pole was approaching fast. I attempted to swerve out of its path when it struck my front end.

21. I was unable to stop in time and my car crashed into the other vehicle. The driver and passenger then left immediately for a holiday with injuries.

*J. John and Mark Stibbe*

Copyright 2004 by Randy Glasbergen.
www.glasbergen.com

**"It's a petition to have chocolate reclassified as a vegetable."**

Did you ever have one of those nights where you didn't want to go out . . . but your hair looked too good to stay home?

*Jack Simmons*

Recently a friend of mine went to a high-priced psychiatrist on Park Avenue in New York City. Once inside
my friend was faced with two doors. One said
"Consultant," the other said, "Analyst." Entering the
door reading "Analyst," my friend encountered two
more doors. One said, "With Couch," the other said
"Without Couch." Entering the door advertising "With
Couch" were two more doors. One read "Really Sick"
and one read "Just Kidding Around." My friend entered
through the door reading "Really Sick" only to find two
more doors. One read "Income over $50,000 a year"
and the other read "Income under $50,000 a year." My
friend entered the door reading "Under $50,000 a
year" . . . and found himself back on Park Avenue.

*Executive Speechwriter Newsletter*

## JUST ASKING

Speaking of logical questions . . .

Why is the third hand on the watch called the
second hand?

If a word is misspelled in the dictionary, how would
we ever know?

Why do *tug*boats *push* their barges?

Why do "slow down" and "slow up" mean the same thing?

Why do we say something is out of whack?
What is a whack?

Why do "fat chance" and "slim chance" mean the
same thing?

Why are they called "stands" when they are made
for sitting?

Why is it called "after dark" when it is really "after light?"

Why are "wise man" and "wise guy" opposites?

Why do "overlook" and "oversee" mean opposite
things?

Why is phonics not spelled the way it sounds?

How can you lose your life's savings on something
called securities?

Why do you press harder on the buttons of a remote
control when you know the batteries are dead?

Why do we wash bath towels? Aren't we clean when
we use them?

Why is the time of day with the slowest traffic called
rush hour?

If procrastinators had a club, would they ever have
a meeting?

Why is there always one in every crowd?

If work is so terrific, why do they have to pay you to do it?

Have you ever noticed that just one letter makes all the difference between here and there?

If the #2 pencil is the most popular, why is it still #2?

Why do we sing "Take Me Out to the Ballgame" when we're already there?

Isn't it strange that the same people who laugh at gypsy fortune-tellers take economists seriously?

If practice makes perfect, and nobody's perfect, why practice?

If the world's a stage, where does the audience sit?

Who decided that Hotpoint would be a good name for a company that sells refrigerators?

*Bernard Brunsting*

**He was standing at Death's door, and the doctor was trying to pull him through.**

*Author unknown*

## I'LL BE SEEING YOU

My friend Lee Nelson is a funeral director for a prestigious chain of funeral homes in our area. One day he received a death call and went to pick up a deceased woman at a local hospital. The next day the woman's family came in to make arrangements for her funeral.

Lee related what happened as he was assisting them in making the final choices for their mother's service.

"Do you have an article of jewelry or clothing that you would like to have put on your mother during the service and then removed before the interment?" asked Lee.

Thinking for a moment, the daughter said, "Yes . . . yes I do." And she began digging around in her purse while Lee waited patiently.

Finally, she opened a small change purse and took something out, holding it out to Lee in her closed hand. Lee held out his hand, expecting to receive a necklace or some other piece of jewelry, but when he opened his hand, the dead woman's glass eye was staring at him.

Shocked and a little repulsed, Lee quietly put the glass eye down on the desk, stood up slowly, and said, "Would you please excuse me for a minute?" Then he left the room to try and recompose himself.

Out in the lobby of the funeral home, he related what had happened to his supervisor and the receptionist, and they all had a good laugh. Lee says it took him about ten minutes to regain his composure so he could go back into the office and help the family finish the arrangements.

He walked down the hall and had his hand on the office doorknob when his supervisor stopped him.

With a serious look on his face, he said, "Lee, did the family tell you what the mother's final words were?"

"No," said Lee.

"She said, 'I'll keep an eye out for you!'"

Lee said it took him another ten minutes to recover from that remark before he could face the family again and complete his task.

*H. Lee Nelson*

## REAL HEADLINES

Following are actual headlines that have appeared in print:

Include Your Children When Baking Cookies

Police Begin Campaign to Run Down Jaywalkers

Safety Experts Say School Bus Passengers Should Be Belted

Drunk Gets Nine Months in Violin Case

Survivor of Siamese Twins Joins Parents

Farmer Bill Dies in House

Iraqi Head Seeks Arms

British Left Waffles on Falkland Islands

Lung Cancer in Women Mushrooms

Eye Drops Off Shelf

Teacher Strikes Idle Kids

Squad Helps Dog Bite Victim

Enraged Cow Injures Farmer with Ax

Plane Too Close to Ground, Crash Probe Told

Juvenile Court to Try Shooting Defendant

Two Soviet Ships Collide, One Dies

Killer Sentenced to Die for Second Time in 10 Years

Cold Wave Linked to Temperatures

Enfields Couple Slain; Police Suspect Homicide

Red Tape Holds Up New Bridge

Deer Kill 17,000

Typhoon Rips through Cemetery; Hundreds Dead

Man Struck by Lightning Faces Battery Charge

New Study of Obesity Looks for Larger Test Group

Kids Make Nutritious Snacks

Chef Throws His Heart into Helping Feed Needy

Arson Suspect Is Held in Massachusetts Fire

British Union Finds Dwarfs in Short Supply

Lansing Residents Can Drop Off Trees

Local High School Dropouts Cut in Half

New Vaccine May Contain Rabies

Deaf College Opens Doors to Hearing

Air Head Fired

Steals Clock, Faces Time

Old School Pillars Are Replaced by Alumni

Bank Drive-in Window Blocked by Board

Hospitals Are Sued by 7 Foot Doctors

*Compiled from Public Records*

"Hey, look! The road to heaven is paved with good intentions too."

Humor is a divine quality, and God has the greatest
sense of humor of all. He must have; otherwise He
wouldn't have made so many politicians.

*Dr. Martin Luther King Jr.*

## INFORMATION GAP

One of President Reagan's favorite stories was about
the congressman who each election year would visit
his district's poor Indian reservation and promise better
housing and more jobs. After every speech, the Indians
would shout, "Oohglah. Oohglah."

It wasn't until one time when the Indian chief was
leading him over to a horse so he could put on an Indian
headdress and pose for a photo opportunity, that the congressman was clued in. When he neared the steed, the
chief called out to him, "Careful, Congressman, don't step
in the ooglah!"

*Executive Speechwriter Newsletter*

The National Park Service decided to install toilets for backpackers on the Appalachian Trail.
One toilet, five miles from the highway on a
mountaintop, had to be equipped with wheelchair
ramps to conform to government regulations.

*Dr. Lawrence J. Peter*

## YOU DON'T KNOW ME, BUT . . .

I was traveling on a bus one day in the 1980s, and a lady, who was headmistress of the local school, got on the bus. She sat down next to a very respectable town attorney and electrified the whole busload of passengers by saying to him, "I can see you don't know who I am, but you are the father of one of my children."

*Edward Gosse*

A worker was called on the carpet by his supervisor for talking back to his foreman. "Is it true that you called him a liar?"

"Yes, I did."

"Did you call him stupid?"

"Yes."

"And did you call him an opinionated, bull-headed egomaniac?"

"No, but would you write that down so I can remember it?"

*Bob Phillips*

## BURGERS, FAST FOOD AND GOD:
## LIVING ON A WING AND A PRAYER

When the Mongols were busy murdering and pillaging during the Middle Ages, little did they realize the magnitude of inventing steak tartare, ground meat that eventually became what we know as hamburger. The irony is that hundreds of years later, the only people who can understand the language being spoken through the drive-through speaker at a fast-food restaurant are Mongols. We can put people on other planets, but they had better not try to order a corn dog.

The conversation usually goes something like this:

Speaker: "Welcome to Burger/Taco/Chicken World. Would you like to mambo?"

Me: "What? I don't dance."

Speaker: "What? I asked if you would like one of our combos."

Me: "Oh. Sorry. No, I'll just have a cheeseburger."

Speaker: "I'm sorry. We don't have cheese burners."

Me: "What? I said *cheeseburger!*"

Speaker: "Oh, sorry. Would you like to catch up?"

Me: "I didn't know I was behind."

Speaker: "I'm sorry, sir. We don't have any beehives, only honey barbecue sauce."

Me: "What? You asked me if I wanted to catch up."

Speaker: "No, sir. I asked if you wanted ketchup on your cheeseburner."

At this point in the conversation I am becoming a fan of canned soup. Out of angry determination I continue.

Me: "Do you have chicken legs?"

Speaker: "I used to, but I've been working out."

Me: "What? Look, read my lips. Give me a chicken dinner."

Speaker: "Have you had a chicken strip?"

Me: "No, I had one that danced funny, but what's that got to do with anything?"

Speaker: "I asked if you had tried our chicken strips."

Me: "Oh, for crying out loud! Give me some cheese dip!"

Speaker: "Sir, it's nacho cheese."

Me: "I know! It's for my wife!"

Speaker: "What?"

I am fully convinced that if Jesus had been forced to place His order through a fast-food drive-through speaker, then the real miracle at the feeding of the five thousand would have been how that many people could be filled by two gloves and a dish.

*Martin Babb*

God always answers prayers.
Sometimes it's yes.
Sometimes the answer is no.
Sometimes it's
"You've gotta be kidding!"

*President Jimmy Carter*

# 2

# A View from the Pew

*There's just nothing quite as funny as the holy
mishappenings in church when you're not supposed to laugh. When something goes religiously
wrong, it doesn't just go slightly wrong, it goes
hysterically wrong.*

## THE GREAT PEW INVASION

I noticed it the minute I walked into the sanctuary that
Sunday, but by then it was too late. There wasn't a thing I
could do about it. My heart began to pound, my knees wobbled,
and I broke into a cold sweat and started hyperventilating.

Someone was sitting in my pew.

Okay, so it wasn't *really* my pew. I didn't pay for it or
anything like that. It didn't have my nameplate on it. (It
used to, but the ushers made me take it down.)

Still, it was *my* pew. Everyone knew it was my pew. It
was where I always sat—third row from the back on the
left-hand side.

The Phillips family sat in the third row from the back on

the right-hand side. I'd never dream of sitting in their pew. Not again, anyway. I tried that once, but as soon as the pastor asked the congregation to stand, the Phillipses slid in behind me and forced me to relocate. (Unfortunately, this sort of pew-jacking is quite common in many churches.)

The Randolph family had homesteaded the front row, center section, and they didn't take any chances. Each and every Sunday they'd arrive at church an hour early just to rope off their pew. That in itself may sound reasonable, but I still say those security guards they posted at each end were a bit much.

Mr. Carter claimed the fourth row from the front, right-hand section, aisle seat. Once, an usher tried to persuade him to scoot down in order to leave room for latecomers, but he merely took out his wallet and produced pictures of his father sitting in that seat, his grandfather sitting in that seat, and his great-grandfather sitting in that seat. The way he figured it, that seat was a family heirloom and he wasn't about to give it up.

The above cases may sound extreme, but if you've studied Pew Theory as I have (I did my thesis on it), you'll find pew possessiveness is not unusual. Thousands of regular church attendees have their chosen pews—pews which took weeks, months, perhaps even years to stake out.

Selecting the family pew is no simple undertaking. The perfect pew must have the perfect location. If you happen to select a pew that's under a heating duct, you could find yourself breaking out into a sweat even when the pastor *isn't* preaching on tithing. But you don't want it under an air condi-

tioning vent either, or icicles could start forming on your hym-
nal and the membership might think you're a little strange for
keeping your choir robe on throughout the entire service.

Another consideration in pew selection is the cushion. It
needs to have just the right "give."
Surveys have shown that the ideal pew
cushion is one which would allow you to
sit tall when the pastor is praising the
congregation on their faithfulness but to
sink down three or four inches when he
begins the building-fund pledge drive.

> They were all
> a part of God's
> house, and one
> wasn't any better
> than the next.

However, a pew cushion that's too
soft and comfortable may not be a good
idea. Halfway through the service, you could become drowsy,
lose your mental alertness, and end up volunteering to be the
church newsletter editor, serve as youth camp counselor and
teach the three-year-olds' Sunday school class—all with one
yawn and the inadvertent stretching of your arm upward.

I had considered all these points when I made my pew
selection. My pew of choice wasn't too soft or too hard. It
wasn't too hot or too cold. It was perfect. But now, all I could
do was stand by helplessly while someone was shamelessly
trespassing—invading my territory, jumping my claim.

Seeing the disbelief on my face and fearing I might faint
from the shock, an usher quickly led me to the tenth row,
center section.

"It'll be all right," he smiled, patting my hand reassur-
ingly. "Maybe you'll get your favorite pew back next week."

Wait a minute, I thought to myself. Next week? My pew wasn't on a time-share program. It had been my pew every Sunday as long as I could remember. There wasn't any room for compromise here.

"Come on, cheer up," he continued, handing me a Sunday bulletin. "Who knows? You may end up liking this pew even better."

Obviously, he didn't understand. I couldn't forget my old pew that easily. That pew and I had been through a lot together. It had been there for me through the ups and downs of the song services. It had endured all my fidgeting during those annual stewardship sermons. It had heard every prayer I had prayed and had absorbed every tear I had cried. It knew me and I knew it. I knew the exact location of each loose thread in the upholstery. I had memorized the pattern of the nicks in the wood trim. There was no way I could turn my back on it now.

I pouted during the announcements and gritted my teeth while the congregation sang "I Surrender All." I tried singing along, but I couldn't. I was afraid my "all" might include my pew, and I wasn't sure I was ready for such a sacrifice.

Somehow, though, by the close of the service that sacrifice didn't seem so great. To my amazement, I discovered that my new pew was every bit as comfortable as my old one and even had something my former pew didn't have—a brand new family who had been wanting to become more involved in the church. I had the opportunity to meet them and encourage them to attend some upcoming events.

The following Sunday the ushers once again filled my old pew, forcing me to sit in the eighth row, left-hand section. There, I met a lady who was going through a difficult situation similar to one I had faced a few years earlier. I was able to get to know her as well and tell her about the reality of God's faithfulness and love.

After a few more Sundays away from my pew, it no longer mattered where I sat—in the front, in the back, on the right side, or left side. I enjoyed every pew. They were all a part of God's house, and one wasn't any better than the next.

Now granted, you won't see The Great Pew Invasion mentioned in the history books, and the subject doesn't come up much at the Pentagon, but it was an important event in my life.

Now, when the ushers ask me to scoot down a few seats, instead of digging in my heels and singing "I Shall Not Be Moved," I look them right in the eye and sing "I'll Go Where You Want Me to Go."

*Martha Bolton*

## OUR CHURCH WILL BE PERFECT WHEN WE HEAR . . .

"Hey! It's my turn to sit in the front pew."

"I was so enthralled, I never noticed your sermon went twenty-five minutes overtime."

"Personally, I find witnessing much more enjoyable than golf."

"I dearly want to be a teacher in the junior high Sunday school class."

"Forget the denominational minimum salary; let's pay our pastor so he can live like we do."

"I love it when we sing hymns I've never heard before."

"Since we're all here, let's start the service early."

"Nothing inspires me and strengthens my commitment like our annual stewardship campaign."

"Pastor, we'd like to send you to this continuing-education seminar in the Bahamas."

"I've decided to give our church the five hundred dollars a month I used to send to TV evangelists."

*The World's Greatest Collection of Church Jokes*

"It's the last time I fill out a visitor's card."

A young man entered the convention hall where a religious gathering was being held. He spotted one empty aisle seat near the front. "Is this chair saved?" he asked the man sitting next to the empty chair.

"I'm not sure," he responded, "but sit down and we'll pray for it together."

*J. M. Braude*

## CELEBRATE TOGETHER

Jack became a Christian on Sunday. On Wednesday afternoon his wife Carol gave birth to a beautiful baby girl. Jack, a big, burly guy who had a gruff voice and a flamboyant manner, was thrilled. And he wanted to tell somebody.

The church met on Wednesday evening for Bible study. So, being excited about his new daughter and his new church family at the same time, naturally Jack thought we would all want to hear the good news.

There was a side entrance to the auditorium where the adult class met. When you came in that door, you were standing in front of the audience for all to see. Ron, the local minister, had just stood up to begin the Bible study when Jack burst in the side door beaming and announced for all the world to hear, "It's a girl!"

There were a few muffled giggles, but everyone basically reacted happily. Then Jack bounced past Ron and politely hoisted himself up to sit on top of the communion table, bringing gasps from the conservative group in the rear of the auditorium. Jack was oblivious to anything beyond his exuberance and proceeded to give us a blow-by-blow account of the day's events. Meanwhile, Ron, a highly dignified white-shirt-navy-suit kind of minister, was quickly turning ashen, not quite knowing how to stop Jack politely.

To top off his big announcement, Jack hopped down off the "holy" table and bounded up and down the aisles, handing out cigars to all the men and candy to all the ladies. The first cigar went to Ron, whose face instantly flushed from ash to scarlet. And the gasps from the back erupted and then lapsed into shocked silence. I collapsed in laughter on the second pew.

Then, as suddenly as he had burst into the room, Jack was gone—back to the hospital to be with Carol and Super Baby. He didn't even stay for Bible study.

When the guffaws and gasps died down, I glanced up to see Ron still standing in front of the class with his Bible in one hand and the cigar in the other. His feet were frozen in place, and he couldn't, for the life of him, figure out what to say. Finally, with obvious fluster and fumbling, he stuck the cigar in his inside coat pocket and said, "I'll just put this away so no one will smoke it."

At that point I couldn't control myself any longer, so I escaped to the ladies' room where I went into hysterics. I'm sure the good Lord was laughing too.

Here's the point: hallelujah happenings shouldn't receive

ho-hum responses. Way to go, Jack. Thanks for loosening our spiritual ties a bit.

*Mary Hollingsworth*

A woman died and went to heaven. At the pearly gates, St. Peter was quizzing the new arrivals. "Before you may enter, can you tell me God's first name?" he asked. After thinking a moment, the woman smiled and said, "Andy?" "Andy?" St. Peter replied, "Where'd you get Andy?" "We sang it in church all the time: 'Andy walks with me, Andy talks with me, Andy tells me I am His own . . . '"

*Lowell D. Streiker*

## NOT LEARNED AT CHURCH

A cat and a mouse died on the same day and went up to heaven. While strolling down the golden street they met God, and He asked them, "How do you like it so far?"

The mouse replied, "It's great, but can I have a pair of in-line skates?"

God said, "Sure," and He gave the mouse the skates.

Next day God saw the cat and asked him, "How do you like it up here so far?"

The cat replied, "Great, I didn't know you had Meals on Wheels."

*The World's Greatest Collection of Church Jokes*

"Don't push your luck."

## APPLE THEOLOGY

I celebrate Easter with 1.5 billion other Christian brothers and sisters across the globe. It's around this time of year that one of the most vivid of my church recollections flashes in front of my mind's eye over and over again.

The preacher (whose name I cannot recall) had just given a powerful message about how the human spirit can be perpetually renewed by God's Spirit. It was a magnificent display of the oratorical genius that has long been a part of the Afro-Christian tradition—the rhythmic cadences, the lucid and lyrical language, punctuated with anecdotes that highlight the tragi-comedy of everyday life.

"I am going to end this morning by telling you something that happened when I was in seminary," he said, dabbing his forehead with a white handkerchief that had been folded into a perfect square.

"I went to the University of Chicago Divinity School. Every year they used to have what was called 'Baptist Day.'

It was a day when they invited the entire Baptist community in the area to visit the school, basically because they wanted the Baptist dollars to keep coming in," he explained.

"On this day everyone was to bring a bag lunch to be eaten outdoors in a grassy picnic area, giving the students, faculty and visitors a chance to mingle.

"And every 'Baptist Day' the school would invite one of the greatest minds in theological education to give a lecture. This one year the great Paul Tillich came to speak."

The preacher paused to sip some water.

"Dr. Tillich spoke for two-and-a-half hours, proving that the historical Resurrection was false. He quoted scholar after scholar and book after book, concluding that since there was no such thing as the historical Resurrection, the African American religious tradition was groundless, emotional mumbo-jumbo, because it was based on a relationship with Jesus, who, in fact, never rose from the dead in any literal sense."

The preacher told us that Dr. Tillich ended his talk with a sweeping, "Are there any questions?"

The silence in the packed lecture hall was deafening.

Then, finally, after about thirty seconds—it seemed like five minutes—an old, dark-skinned preacher with a head full of short-cropped woolly white hair stood up in the back of the auditorium.

"Docta Tillich, I got a question," he said as all eyes turned toward him. He reached into his bag lunch and pulled out an apple.

"Docta Tillich . . ." Crunch, munch, munch, munch . . .

"Now, I ain't never read them books you read . . ." Crunch, munch, munch, munch . . . "And I can't recite the Scriptures in the original Greek . . ." Crunch, munch, munch, munch . . . "I don't know nothin' about Niebuhr and Heidegger. . ." Crunch, munch, munch, munch . . .

He finished the apple. Then he began to lick his fingertips and pick his teeth.

"All I wanna know is: This apple I just ate—was it bitter or sweet?"

Dr. Tillich paused for a moment and answered in exemplary scholarly fashion: "I cannot possibly answer that question, for I haven't tasted your apple."

The white-haired preacher dropped the core of his apple into his crumpled paper bag, looked up at Dr. Tillich, and said calmly, "Neither have you tasted my Jesus."

The one-thousand-plus in attendance could not contain themselves.

The auditorium erupted with roaring laughter, cheers, and applause. Paul Tillich promptly thanked his audience and left the lectern.

*Sean Gonsalves*

After unsuccessfully trying to recruit volunteers for a recent church project, our program coordinator put down the phone and said, "Not only are we couch potatoes, but we're pew potatoes, and we're raising tater tots!"

*John C. Cripps*

A college drama group presented a play during which one character stands on a trapdoor and announces, "I descend into hell!" A stagehand below would then pull a rope, the trapdoor would open, and the character would plunge through. The play was well-received.

When the actor playing the part became ill, another actor who was quite overweight took his place. When the new actor announced, "I descend into hell!" the stagehand pulled the rope, and the actor began his plunge, but became hopelessly stuck. No amount of tugging on the rope could make him descend.

One student in the balcony jumped up and yelled, "Hallelujah! Hell is full!"

*Author unknown*

"Good news, Pastor Bob! The overflowing baptistry put out the fire in the sanctuary!"

## GOD'S DRIVER

A limo driver is dispatched to the airport to drive the Pope to his hotel.

After getting all the Pope's luggage loaded in the limo (and His Holiness didn't travel light), the driver notices that the Pope is still standing on the curb.

"Excuse me, Your Holiness," says the driver, "would you please take your seat so we can leave?"

"Well, to tell you the truth," says the Pope, "they never let me drive at the Vatican, and I'd really like to drive today."

"I'm sorry but I cannot let you do that. I'd lose my job! And what if something should happen?" protests the driver, wishing he'd never gone to work that morning.

"There might be something extra in it for you," says the Pope.

Reluctantly, the driver gets in the back as the Pope climbs in behind the wheel. The driver quickly regrets his decision when, after exiting the airport, the Supreme Pontiff floors it, accelerating the limo to 105 mph.

"Please slow down, Your Holiness!" pleads the worried driver, but the Pope keeps the pedal to the metal until they hear sirens.

"Oh, wonderful. Now I'm really going to lose my license," moans the driver.

The Pope pulls over and rolls down the window as the policeman approaches, but the officer takes one look at him, goes back to his motorcycle and gets on the radio.

"I need to talk to the Chief," he says to the dispatcher.

The Chief gets on the radio and the officer tells him that he's stopped a limo going 105 mph.

"So bust him," said the Chief.

"I don't think we want to do that—he's really important," said the policeman.

"All the more reason."

"No, I mean really important."

"Who've you got there, the Mayor?"

"Bigger."

"The President?"

"Bigger."

"Well," said the Chief, "who is it?"

"I think it's God!"

"What makes you think it's God?"

"Well, He's got the Pope driving for Him!"

*J. John and Mark Stibbe*

A minister asked a little girl what she thought of her first church service.

"The music was nice," she said, "but the commercial was too long."

*Bob Phillips*

A little boy returning home from his first circus, comments, "Once you've been to a circus, you'll never enjoy church again."

*J. M. Braude*

## WHERE IS GOD?

A couple had two little boys, ages eight and ten, who were excessively mischievous. The two were always getting into trouble and their parents could be assured that if any mischief occurred in their town their two young sons were in some way involved. The parents were at their wits' end as to what to do about their sons' behavior.

The mother had heard that a clergyman in town had been successful in disciplining children in the past, so she asked her husband if he thought they should send the boys to speak with the clergyman. The husband said, "We might as well. We need to do something before I really lose my temper!" The clergyman agreed to speak with the boys, but asked to see them individually.

The eight-year-old went to meet with him first. The clergyman sat the boy down and asked him sternly, "Where is God?"

The boy made no response, so the clergyman repeated the question in an even sterner tone, "Where is God?"

Again the boy made no attempt to answer. So the clergyman raised his voice even more and shook his finger in the boy's face, "WHERE IS GOD?"

At that the boy bolted from the room and ran straight home, slamming himself in the closet.

His older brother followed him into the closet and said, "What happened?"

The younger brother replied, "We are in BIG trouble this time. God is missing and they think we did it."

*J. John and Mark Stibbe*

JAPHETH! SHEM! MOVE THE HIPPOS AND ELEPHANTS TO THE FRONT!!

## THE OLD SANCTUARY

Our shoutin' Baptist church back home in Houston, Texas, didn't have pews. It had individual seats.

It was a fan-shaped church, which I think is kind of cool, because everybody is closer to the preacher. In long, skinny churches, you can be back so far that you spend the whole time squinting.

But our church was like a real auditorium with individual pull-down seats and armrests. Of course, that meant if you're too fat you couldn't come to our church or else you'd be carrying part of it home with you when you left.

Plus those seats would pop you in the rear when you stood up, so you had to be quick.

If you were skinny and quick, you were welcome at our church.

If I ever build a church, I'm not going to have the same kind of seats. I'm putting in La-Z-Boys with Big Gulp holders and a remote control. I figure, if you're going to sleep, you might as well enjoy it.

Amen, brother.

*Mark Lowry*

## KIDS OFF TRACK

Kids statements that are a little . . . off track:

God bless America thru the night with a light from a bulb!

Oh Susanna, oh don't you cry for me, for I come from Alabama with a Band-Aid on my knee!

Give us this day our deli bread! Glory be to the Father and to the Son and to the Whole East Coast.

We shall come to Joyce's bringing in the cheese.

Gladly, the cross-eyed bear.

"Rex is chewing the paraffin."

Yield not to Penn Station.

Dust Around the Throne

Praise God from whom all blessings flow,
Praise Him all creatures, HERE WE GO!

Olive, the other reindeer, used to laugh and
call him names.

While shepherds washed their socks by night.

He socked me and boxed me with His redeeming glove.

Bringing in the sheets, bringing in the sheets;
we shall come rejoicing bringing in the sheets.


Do your givin' while you're livin', then you're knowin'
where it's goin.'
                                          *Author unknown*


## ON ENVYING THE METHODISTS

Pastor, it's about time for the service to begin," one of the associate ministers said through the closed door of the baptismal dressing room.

"Almost ready," I replied as I hurriedly pulled on the rubber waders that most Baptist preachers use. I reached for a spotless white robe neatly hanging on the rack, put it on, and zipped it up, breathing a sigh of relief that the zipper didn't catch in the fabric. This was one baptism that should be smooth and perfect.

I remembered with gratitude the events that had led to this very moment.

Carol Brady, an attractive young adult, had indicated a strong desire to join our church. Her husband and other members of the family were already members and vitally involved in the programs and ministries of Wilshire. Carol liked everything she knew about the church and was quick to pass this along to others—everything, that is, except baptism.

This was her "big-time hang-up" as she put it. The thought of putting on a robe, stepping into a big "tub" (again, her word) and being immersed before the entire congregation was too much for her.

The more I tried to reassure her, the more nervous she seemed to become. I tried gentle persuasion, understanding, and a touch of firmness, but it got us nowhere.

"Okay, Carol," I said one day, "we've about talked this subject to death. I'll leave the matter with you. If and when you are ready to be baptized, just let me know. Meanwhile, we'll let it rest here for a while."

"Agreed," she responded.

Several weeks went by and the subject was not mentioned by either of us. I determined to give her all the freedom she needed to reach her own decision.

One Friday morning my telephone rang. Carol had only one crisp statement: "Fill the baptistry!"

"When?"

"This Sunday night!"

"It's done."

"And, Bruce," she added, "do it right. A lot of my family and friends will be there."

Now, Sunday night had come and the moment had arrived. The last preparations had taken place. I glanced down again at the waders, smoothed the wrinkles out of the white robe, and waited impatiently for the conclusion of the first congregational hymn. I knew that Carol was waiting in the ladies' drawing room on the other side, preparing to descend the steps into the water to finalize her long and difficult decision.

> Carol had only one crisp statement: "Fill the baptistry!"

*It will all be over in five minutes,* I thought. *Carol will be glad, her friends and family will be happy for her, and I'll be relieved.*

The last note of the hymn had been sung. This was my cue. I opened the door, entered a small hallway, made a right turn, and started down the stairs into the water.

One . . . two . . . three . . . steps.

I froze.

No water. Absolutely bone dry, like a desert.

Carol was halfway down the steps on the opposite side, facing me and giving me this "what-do-I-do-now?" look.

*Good question,* I thought. *What do we do now?*

Slowly I walked to the center of the empty baptistry and made some weak, lame apology about "breakdown in communications." With a painfully forced smile, I then added some inane comment like, "These things just happen in the best of situations."

Out of sight of the congregation, Carol covered her face, snickered, and headed quickly for the ladies' dressing room.

As the next hymn was announced, I slowly ascended the dry steps on my side of the baptistry.

I paused at the top, also out of view of the congregation, looked down at the large, empty tank, and mumbled a prayer:

"Lord, if it's all the same to you, just now I think I'd rather be a Methodist!"

*Bruce McIver*

"...GOLD, FRANKINCENSE AND MYRRH?...I BET HE *REALLY*
WANTED A PUPPY."

## NO LAUGHING ON SUNDAY

Sundays and laws seem to go together. In almost every state of the Union, in small villages and large cities, one

can find archaic ordinances governing Sabbath behavior—
laws that are still on the books.

Pocataligo, Georgia—No dog shall be in a public place
on Sunday without its master on a leash.

Hickory Plains, Arkansas—No female wearing a
nightgown can be rescued by a firefighter while church
services are being held in the community. She must be
fully dressed before she is saved.

Upperville, Virginia—Doctors practicing in this
community have a special responsibility. An unusual
piece of legislation says every woman must "be found to
be wearing a corset" when attending church. A physician
is required to inspect each female in the congregation.

Hillsboro, Oregon—When the citizens here became
fed up with being rudely awakened on Sunday
mornings by crowing chickens, a unique law was
passed. A rooster can still crow on the Sabbath, but
the crowing must be done three hundred or more feet
away from "any house inhabited by human beings."
Let's hope those Oregon roosters can read.

Peewee, West Virginia—It is unlawful for horses to
sleep in the bathtub on Sunday . . . unless the rider
climbs into the tub and sleeps with the horse. Whereas
in Cobre, Nevada, horses may not sleep in bakeries on
Sunday. They don't say anything about people.

Redbush, Kentucky—No citizen may be seen riding an "ugly horse" to church on Sunday.

Ledyard, Connecticut—Local lawmakers passed a special ordinance banning all turtle races on Sunday within the city limits.

Bluff, Utah—Ministers are prohibited from eating onions between the hours of 7:00 AM and 7:00 PM on the Sabbath. And in Wakefield, Rhode Island, citizens aren't allowed to attend a church service within four hours after having eaten garlic.

Indio, California—If you are a fashion-conscious Christian woman who likes to wear a pair of glamorous high heels to church, be careful in Indio. A special law regulates the heel height of shoes worn on the Sabbath. Heels can measure no more than one-and-a-half inches.

Crawford, Nebraska—Any unattached woman caught parachuting on Sunday can be arrested, fined, and given a jail term.

Sutherland, Iowa—It's a violation of the local law for any citizen to carry an ice cream cone in his pocket when he goes to church.

Rawlins, Wyoming—No one is allowed to duel on church grounds when the opponents select anything other than water pistols as weapons.

Kidderville, New Hampshire—Citizens are prohibited from "sticking out a tongue" in the direction of a dog while on the way to church.

Cotton Valley, Louisiana—A teenager can be arrested in Cotton Valley if "silly and/or insulting faces" are made at other teenagers while in Sunday school.

Ryan Crossroads, Alabama—Never eat peanuts while attending church in this town. The pastor has the legal right to make offenders stand in a corner or leave the church until the service is finished.

Colby, Kansas—Men are prohibited from "turning and looking at a woman in that way" on Sunday. If an unfortunate scofflaw gets caught a second time, he has to "wear horse blinders" for a twenty-four-hour period when in public.

Lowes Crossroads, Delaware—Boisterous adults as well as children can be penalized if they "laugh out loud" during a church service.

Bourbon, Mississippi—No married woman is allowed to go out in public on the Sabbath unless she "is properly looked after." How? Her mate must follow twenty paces behind. He's also required to carry a loaded "musket over his left shoulder."

*Robert W. Pelton*

Most people want to serve God, but only in an advisory capacity.

*Author unknown*

## FOR WHOM THE BELL . . .

A minister is walking down the street one sunny afternoon when he notices a very small boy trying to press a doorbell on a house across the street. But the doorbell is too high for the little boy to reach.

After watching the boy's efforts, the minister decides to give the lad a hand. So he crosses over and goes up to the house and gives the bell a solid ring.

Crouching down to the little boy's level, the minister smiles benevolently and asks, "And now what, my little man?"

To which the boy replies, "Now we run!"

*The World's Greatest Collection of Church Jokes*

## A GRAVESIDE SERVICE

A newly appointed young minister was contacted by the local funeral director to hold a graveside service in a small country cemetery. Because the deceased had no friends or family left, there was to be no funeral, just the committal.

The pastor started to the cemetery early enough, but he soon lost his way, causing him to arrive thirty minutes late.

There was no hearse or funeral director in sight, just the workmen, who were sitting under a tree eating lunch. Moving to the newly dug grave, the minister opened his prayer book and read the service over the vault lid that was in place.

When returning to his car, the preacher overheard one of the workmen say, "Maybe we'd better tell him that's a septic tank."

*The World's Greatest Collection of Church Jokes*

"Thanks for the marriage counseling, Pastor. We feel much better."

# 3

## Parents Wanted!

*Parenting isn't for wimps. It's the toughest job you'll ever love. Your life will be filled with happy days, scary days and hilarious moments. After all, kids are funny. And parenting is often a laughing matter.*

### GET THE KID

Mommy, Mommy, Mommy, Mommy, Mommy, Mommy." Marty's persistence matched his rhythmic tugging on my blouse's hem.

I felt like screaming. In fact, I did.

To a little guy my response was probably similar to the release of Mt. St. Helens as I erupted, "What?"

Why a mother waits so long to respond and allows the repetition to light her lava is beyond me. I only know that after spewing all over him I felt terrible . . . and so did he.

Where did all this volcanic anger come from? I seemed to always be upset at something or someone. Often my reactions were greater than the situation called for. I realized that Marty's little-child ways didn't deserve such strong responses.

Have you ever tried making things right when you know you're wrong but don't know how to admit it or quit it? That was often my frustration with Marty.

I'd send him to his room, leaving me with the realization that his punishment was greater than his crime. Then I'd try to make up by slipping him a Twinkie or playing a game with him. I soon found that Twinkies don't build good bridges of communication—too squishy.

During a prayer time, as I cried out to the Lord for help with my temper, especially with my son, an idea formed that I believe was heaven-sent because it made a difference.

I was to pray with Marty before I administered any form of discipline. Sometimes those prayers sounded strange and strained as I almost shouted, "Dear Lord, help this miserable little boy and help his miserable mommy, who wants so desperately to raise him in a way that would honor You."

By the time I said "amen," I was almost a reasonable person. I was able to see past my emotions and do what was in Marty's best interest.

Sometimes he needed a firm hand, but he was dealt with in love instead of anger, and the moment drew us together instead of tearing us apart. Many times all he needed was time and a mother's tender touch.

But one day that boy really ticked me off! I remember heading across the room for him like a high-speed locomotive, steam coming out all sides. I had one goal and intent—get the kid, get the kid, get the kid!

Just as I loomed over him, his eyes the size of saucers, he held up one hand and yelled, "Let's pray!"

Marty had learned a valuable lesson in life: When Mommy talks to Jesus, we're all a lot better off.

*Patsy Clairmont*

"We're calling him 'Quits!'"

(Reprinted with permission of *Medical Economics*).

## KEEP YOUR PANTS ON

It was one of Mother's hectic days. Her small son, who had been playing outside, came in with his pants torn. "You go right in, remove those pants, and start mending them yourself," she ordered.

Sometime later she went in to see how he was getting along. The torn pants were lying across the chair, and the door to the cellar, usually kept closed, was open. She called down the stairs, loudly and sternly: "Are you running around down there without your pants on?"

"No ma'am," was the deep-voiced reply. "I'm just down here reading your gas meter."

*Michael Hodgin*

## BLOWING A CHANCE ON I-65

I was standing by the side of Interstate 65, somewhere in the middle of Indiana, with six screaming children and a hysterical wife, when I realized I would never achieve every parent's dream.

Earlier in the day, all eight of us piled into the car. I turned on the radio to listen, ironically, to Dr. James Dobson's radio program, *Focus on the Family*. It was a tender interview about parenting. I looked in the rearview mirror and counted six beautiful heads.

Then I did what most people do when they listen to *Focus on the Family*. I imagined what it would be like to be interviewed. I gave great, emotional answers and had Dr. Dobson bawling so hard Mike Trout had to go into the other room for a box of tissues.

The program's theme played, and my wife said, "Their story really makes you think, doesn't it?" She hugged the child buckled between us.

"Yeah," I said, thinking about what I would say on program number two the next day. *If they would only try me once*, I thought, *I would hold the record for consecutive days on the program. I have so much wisdom to share. I have so much parental love and understanding flowing through my veins, it's a shame to let it go to waste.*

Traffic was heavy and huge trucks passed on either side, blowing us back and forth between the white lines. We hit Indiana and settled in for a long night. The kids would fall asleep, and I would drive straight on till morning.

As dusk settled, little stomachs took control of the trip. I heard plaintive cries from the back of the car: Like wayward sheep, the children bleated for a fresh pasture of Happy Meals. Unfortunately, I did not have my rod or my staff to comfort them, so I raised my voice in a shepherdly manner and suggested they be quiet.

One of the little sheep, the oldest, kept bleating. Since she is so much like me, her words stung. She has the ability not just to get under my skin, but also to get under it, stand up, walk around, do a cartwheel and kick my eyeballs. To this day no one remembers what pushed me over the edge, but it had something to do with her "tone" and a general disregard of several "severe bleating warnings." (A "bleating warning" is much more serious than a "bleating watch," according to the National Parent Service.)

I can still remember the look in her eyes when, after several threats of "I'm going to pull this car over," I actually did. I was way over on the grass tilting to the starboard side, but you could still feel the trucks pass, as if they were only inches away.

"Get out," I said. They were the only words I needed.

All the air went out of the car. No one breathed, let alone thought of bleating. You could hear a Cheerio drop.

I stomped to the other side of the car and opened the door. The offending sheep was trying to crawl over her siblings toward me, but crawl is not the right word. She was moving like the blob, taking as long as she could to avert the inevitable confrontation.

I grabbed a leg and pulled. The sheep came out of the car in a breach position, crying.

I honestly do not know what I intended to do at that moment. I wasn't going to spank her; she was too big to spank. I wasn't going to leave her there; it would have been unusually cruel to the wolves. I don't even know if I was going to yell at her because before I could open my mouth, my wife burst from the front passenger side, her hair flopping in the wind. With a shriek, she stepped onto the green Indiana grass and yelled, "Don't hurt my baby! Please don't hurt my baby!"

I stopped and looked around, wondering, *Who is this person and what baby is she talking about?* She grabbed my daughter and it was all over. They hugged each other and cried, and I looked out over the cornfield by the highway. The sun was just dipping below the horizon. I turned to our car. All the windows were down, and I saw five mouths agape.

For the next few miles all I could hear was whimpering

from the backseat. Sheep sometimes safely graze on such experiences.

And then the dawn broke. I looked at my wife and she wiped her eyes. I thought she was crying, but she was stifling a smile.

"What?" I said.

She paused for effect and then said the words I'll never forget.

"I think we just blew our chance to be on *Focus on the Family*."

*Chris Fabry*

"O.K., Sweeties. You're all going to need to go naked for just a day or two till Mommy catches up with the laundry."

An allowance is what you pay your child to live with you.

*Henny Youngman*

## TEN WAYS TO KNOW IF YOU'RE
## READY FOR CHILDREN

1. Women: Put on a dressing gown and tie a beanbag chair around your waist. Leave it there for nine months. After nine months, remove ten percent of the beans.

   Men: Go to the local drugstore and dump the contents of your wallet on the counter. Tell the pharmacists to help themselves. Then go to the supermarket and arrange to have your paycheck directly deposited into the store's account.

2. Find parents with children who misbehave and offer them advice about child rearing and discipline. Enjoy the experience. It will be the last time you'll have all the answers.

3. To discover how the nights will feel after you have a baby, set your alarm to go off every two hours between 10:00 PM and 5:00 AM. Each time you get out of bed, carry around a wet bag weighing eight to twelve pounds. Sing songs and jiggle the bag. At 5:00 AM, get up and make breakfast while trying to look cheerful. Keep this up for five years.

4. To anticipate the messes made by children, smear peanut butter and jelly on your sofa and curtains. Shove a mini pizza into your VCR. Take potting soil

from your household plants and apply it directly to your wallpaper. Using crayons, draw hundreds of uneven circles on the lower part of your living-room walls. Now stand back and smile as you survey the scene.

5. To prepare for dressing small children, go to your local pet store and purchase a medium-sized octopus. Practice putting the octopus into a sandwich-sized zipper bag without any arms sticking out. Time allowed for this: all morning.

6. Trade in your two-door sports car for a minivan. Stick a chocolate ice cream bar in the glove compartment and leave it there all summer. Jam a quarter into the cassette player and smash a family-sized bag of chocolate cookies into the seats and grind them into the carpet with your heel. Then run a garden rake along the sides of the van. Now you have a "family vehicle."

7. Repeat everything you say at least five times—patiently.

8. Visit the local grocery store with the closest thing you can find to a preschool child. A full-grown goat is excellent. If you plan to have more than one child, take more than one goat. Buy your week's groceries without letting the goats out of your sight. Pay for everything the goats eat or destroy. Then herd the

goats and groceries to your chocolate-stained minivan in the parking lot.

9.  Hollow out a melon. Make a small hole in the side. Suspend it from the ceiling and swing it from side to side. Now take a bowl of soggy Froot Loops and attempt to spoon them into the swaying melon by pretending to be an airplane. Continue until half the Froot Loops are gone. Tip the rest into your lap, spilling a large amount on the floor. You're now ready to feed a child.

10.  Finally, think about the proudest moment in your life to date. Perhaps it was graduation or your wedding day or landing that important job. Add to that feeling the sensation you received when you first found out your husband or wife really loved you or when you made your parents proud or when someone looked up to you as a role model. Now multiply those combined feelings of exhilaration by one hundred, and add a broad smile and a chest-bursting sense of pride. If you can barely contain all that excitement and energy, you're ready to have children.

*Stan Toler*

**The thing that impresses me most about America is the way parents obey their children.**

*The Duke of Wellington*

## HOW PARENTHOOD CHANGES WITH
## SUCCEEDING BABIES

*Your Clothes*

1st Baby: You begin wearing maternity clothes as soon as your OB/GYN confirms your pregnancy.

2nd Baby: You wear your regular clothes for as long as possible.

3rd Baby: Your maternity clothes are your regular clothes.

*The Baby's Name*

1st Baby: You pore over baby name books and practice pronouncing and writing combinations of all your favorites.

2nd Baby: Someone has to name their kid after your great-aunt Mavis, right? It might as well be you.

3rd Baby: You open a name book, close your eyes, and see where your finger falls. Bimaldo? Perfect.

*Preparing for the Birth*

1st Baby: You practice your breathing religiously.

2nd Baby: You don't bother practicing because you remember that last time breathing didn't do a thing.

3rd Baby: You ask for an epidural in your eighth month.

### Worries

1st Baby: At the first sign of distress—a whimper, a frown—you pick up the baby.

2nd Baby: You pick the baby up when her wails threaten to wake your firstborn.

3rd Baby: You teach your three-year-old how to rewind the mechanical swing.

### Activities

1st Baby: You take your infant to Baby Gymnastics, Baby Swing and Baby Story Hour.

2nd Baby: You take your infant to Baby Gymnastics.

3rd Baby: You take your infant to the supermarket and the dry cleaner.

### Going Out

1st Baby: The first time you leave your baby with a sitter, you call home five times.

2nd Baby: Just before you walk out the door, you remember to leave a number where you can be reached.

3rd Baby: You leave instructions for the sitter to call only if she sees blood.

*At Home*

1st Baby: You spend a good bit of every day just gazing at the baby.

2nd Baby: You spend a bit of every day watching to be sure your older child isn't squeezing, poking or hitting the baby.

3rd Baby: You spend a little bit of every day hiding from the children.

*Becky Freeman*

**"There! Now you've got no reason to wake us up at 3 A.M. asking for a glass of water."**

The most remarkable thing about my mother is that
for thirty years she served the family nothing but
leftovers. The original meal has never been found.

*Calvin Trillin*


Every mother in the world worries about her children turning into teenagers and staging a family
coup. Not to worry. They don't have the stamina to
take over. They're too sluggish. Their arteries are
clogged with chips and pizza.

I hate those women's magazines with articles
about how to feed a family of six on ninety-six dollars
a month. You show me a woman who can do this, and
I'll show you a woman whose entire family is anorexic.
The way my kids eat, ninety-six dollars gets me down
the first aisle and halfway through the dairy case.

*Kathy Peel*


There's a Spanish story of a father and son who
had become estranged. The son ran away, and the
father set off to find him. He searched for months
to no avail. Finally, in a last desperate effort to find
him, the father put an ad in a Madrid newspaper.
The ad read, "Dear Paco, meet me in front of this
newspaper office at noon on Saturday. All is for-
given. I love you. Your Father."

On Saturday, eight hundred Pacos showed up,
looking for forgiveness and love from their fathers.

*Ernest Hemingway*

## FIRST DATE

On her desk is a calendar with two very important words scrawled under this Friday. It says "Date Night." Friday night is the evening my world comes to an end.

I've been waiting more than thirteen years for this night. I've been dreading it: her first date. I don't mind telling you it scares me, the woman she is becoming. A friend asked if I liked the fellow taking her out, and I replied, "Not particularly." I wanted him to be the perfect person, the perfect date. I suppose he'll have to do.

It only seems like a couple of hours since Andrea and I brought her home from the hospital, and now it's time for her first date. I can still remember holding her in my arms on the first morning of her life. The anticipation, the mystery of having a child, and then the sudden cry and the soiled diaper awakened me to the truth. Old people, people in their forties, told me it would go by fast, and I believed them. But not this fast.

I have been resigned to this inevitability and have tried to let her go a little each day. A choice here or there, whether to let her wear socks with the sandals or get her hair cut short. Last year she wanted another pierce in the ear and red hair. What will it be next year? But those are little changes. What father in his right mind lets his daughter date at thirteen?

Friday afternoon blew by like a hurricane. She was to be ready at 5:15. There was talk of a quick run to a local department store for last-minute details. A buzz skittered among the siblings who wondered in awe as they saw her with a dress and nice shoes. What's up? Why not the shorts and a T-shirt?

The date arrived in his car at 5:16:44. I know because my watch was the only thing I could really focus on. He rang the doorbell and my daughter met him, smiling. He handed her a single rose and placed a bouquet of flowers in the hands of my wife. They both said, "Thank you," and giggled.

He sat in our living room, my wife and daughter gazing intermittently at the date and the ceiling, wondering where he would take her to eat, what movie they would see. And then it was time to leave. Just like that. All the letting go in the universe cannot prepare you for that moment.

My wife stopped them for one last picture, a little water in her eye, and then the door closed and the two were gone.

The date opened the car door for her. He turned the air conditioning on high because he knew she would appreciate it. He does know her quite well. He took her to a restaurant that served steak because he knew she was apprehensive about eating anything you have to cut with a knife and she wanted a little practice. That's what first dates are for. She had never eaten steak before and she was nervous about selecting the correct fork to use for the salad. So he showed her. She ate nearly all of the New York strip but allowed him to finish the potato.

Her date drove her to a theater, and they spent forty-five minutes milling about, laughing, talking, waiting for the movie. They ate Reese's Pieces as they watched a romantic comedy. Then he brought her home.

As they stepped into the house, her date opened his arms, much like he had done thirteen years before, and held her tightly for only a moment. She seemed so close, but at the same time so far away.

And before I went to sleep that night in the room next to hers, I gave thanks to the Father above for tiny hands that grow, for Fridays, for the innocence of daughters, and that I hadn't missed the opportunity to be her first date.

*Chris Fabry*

**The way I look at it, if the kids are still alive when my husband comes home from work, then I've done my job.**

*Roseanne Barr*

### I OWE MY MOTHER!

1. My mother taught me TO APPRECIATE A JOB WELL DONE. "If you're going to kill each other, do it outside. I just finished cleaning."

2. My mother taught me RELIGION. "You'd better pray that will come out of the carpet."

3. My mother taught me about TIME TRAVEL.
   "If you don't straighten up, I'm going to knock you
   into the middle of next week!"

4. My mother taught me LOGIC.
   "Because I said so, that's why."

5. My mother taught me MORE LOGIC.
   "If you fall out of that swing and break your neck,
   you're not going to the store with me."

6. My mother taught me FORESIGHT.
   "Make sure you wear clean underwear, in case
   you're in an accident."

7. My mother taught me IRONY.
   "Keep crying, and I'll give you something
   to cry about."

8. My mother taught me about the science of OSMOSIS.
   "Shut your mouth and eat your supper."

9. My mother taught me about CONTORTIONISM.
   "Will you look at the back of your neck!"

10. My mother taught me about STAMINA.
    "You'll sit there until all that spinach is gone."

11. My mother taught me about WEATHER.
    "This room of yours looks as if a tornado went
    through it."

12. My mother taught me about HYPOCRISY.
    "If I've told you once, I've told you a million times.
    Don't exaggerate!"

13. My mother taught me the CIRCLE OF LIFE.
    "I brought you into this world and I can take you out."

14. My mother taught me about BEHAVIOR
    MODIFICATION. "Stop acting like your father!"

15. My mother taught me about ENVY.
    "There are millions of less fortunate children in this
    world who don't have wonderful parents like you do."

16. My mother taught me about ANTICIPATION.
    "Just wait until we get home."

17. My mother taught me about RECEIVING.
    "You're going to get it when you get home!"

18. My mother taught me MEDICAL SCIENCE.
    "If you don't stop crossing your eyes, they are going
    to freeze that way."

19. My mother taught me ESP.
    "Put your sweater on; don't you think I know when
    you are cold?"

20. My mother taught me HUMOR.
    "When that lawn mower cuts off your toes, don't
    come running to me."

21. My mother taught me HOW TO BECOME AN ADULT. "If you don't eat your vegetables, you'll never grow up."

22. My mother taught me GENETICS.
"You're just like your father."

23. My mother taught me about my ROOTS.
"Shut that door behind you. Do you think you were born in a barn?

24. My mother taught me WISDOM.
"When you get to be my age, you'll understand."

25. And my favorite: My mother taught me about JUSTICE. "One day you'll have kids, and I hope they turn out just like you."

*Author unknown*

Father looking over his son's report card: "One thing is in your favor. With these grades you couldn't possibly be cheating."

*Tal D. Bonham*

I've wanted to run away from home more often since I've had kids than when I was a boy.

*Bob Phillips*

## A WHEELS DEAL

A young boy who had just got his driving license asked his father, who was a minister, if they could discuss the use of the car. His father took him to his study and said to him, "I'll make a deal with you. You bring your grades up, study your Bible a little and get your hair cut and we'll talk about it."

After about a month the boy came back and again asked his father if they could discuss the use of the car. They again went to the father's study where his father said, "Son, I've been real proud of you. You have brought your grades up, you've studied your Bible diligently, but you didn't get your hair cut!"

The young man waited a moment and replied, "You know Dad, I've been thinking about that. You know, Samson had long hair, Moses had long hair, Noah had long hair, and even Jesus had long hair . . ."

To which his father replied, "Yes, and they walked everywhere they went!"

*J. John and Mark Stibbe*

## WITHOUT CHILDREN

What a boring and depressing world this would be without children! Just think, there would be no need for lollipops, cotton candy or licorice. Ponies would be out of work. Amusement parks with carousels would be obsolete.

Santa Claus and the Easter Bunny would have to retire. And nobody would care when a baby robin fell out of its nest.

Infectious giggles would never be heard, and "peek-a-boo" would disappear from the English language. If there were no children, who would make grandparents smile, who would play pat-a-cake, and who would try to whistle with crackers in his mouth? Balloons would never pop, milk would rarely spill, and sticky hands from chocolate bars would be a thing of the past.

Without children, there would be no use for toy trains, dolls that walk and talk, or jack-in-the-boxes. Barney the purple dinosaur would have no one to hug, and Kermit the frog would just turn green and die. Caterpillars wouldn't get stroked, and turtles would never get to sleep in the house. All in all, life would be a real drag.

Let's face it, children are the essence of life. They are God's answer to depression, loneliness and hate. Children are joy and love personified. They are God himself in tiny bodies.

*Mary Hollingsworth*

Mothers give sons permission to be princes, but the fathers must show them how . . . Fathers give daughters permission to be princesses, and mothers must show them how. Otherwise, both boys and girls will grow up and always see themselves as frogs.

*Eric Berne*

Dear Mom and Dad,

Cla$$e$ are really great. I am making lot$ of friend$ and $tudying very hard. I $imply can't think of anything I need, $o if you would like, you can ju$t $end me a card, a$ I would love to hear from you. You're the be$t parent$!

Love,

Your $on

*The reply:*

Dear Son,

We kNOw that astroNOmy, ecoNOmics, and oceaNOgraphy are eNOugh to keep even an hoNOr student busy. Do NOt forget that the pursuit of kNOwledge is a NOble task.

Will we see you in NOvember? We enjoyed getting your letter. Write aNOther one when you get some time.

Love,

Mom and Dad

*Jennifer Harlin*

"Let's try getting up every night at 2:00 AM to feed the cat. If we enjoy doing that, then we can talk about having a baby."

If you hear the toilet flush and the word *uh-oh*, it's already too late.

Nancy Kennedy

Two little boys came bursting into the house, shouting to their mother that the youngest brother had fallen into the lake.

"We tried giving him artificial respiration," one of them gulped, "but he kept getting up and running away."

Tal D. Bonham

## NOTHING DOING

What is it about children and bathrooms? All I know is that a bathroom door closed longer than five minutes is reason for suspicion. Take a typical bathroom door conversation with Laura at age four.

"Laura, what are you doing in there?"

"Nothing."

"Can you unlock the door, so Mommy can see?"

"Not yet. I'm busy."

"What are you busy doing?"

"Nothing."

In the past, I've discovered "nothing" to be two dozen unwrapped bars of soap, an entire roll of toilet paper unrolled into a heap on the floor, Vaseline smeared on the mirror, and a Teddy bear taking a bubble bath in the toilet.

Those things I learned to live with. It was the combined sounds of flushing and giggling that cause me to panic. Echoes of "Mommy, look at my shoe spin!" and "Bye-bye toothbrush!" still haunt me.

However, a four-year-old is nothing compared to an eight-year-old. An eight-year-old doing "nothing" in the bathroom is lying. Eight-year-olds shave their arms and try to pierce their own ears with a paper clip. They poke hundreds of tiny holes in the toothpaste tube and they cut their own hair—badly.

But at least eight-year-olds don't spend every waking moment in the bathroom like teenage girls do. When a teenage girl says she's doing "nothing" in the bathroom, she's doing exactly that—and it takes her an hour and a half to do it. Every hair has to be in place, every blemish on her face must be inspected . . . and cried over. Prayers must be offered up over a too-flat chest and too-wide hips.

When you ask, "What are you doing in there?" she replies, "Nothing! Can't everybody leave me alone?! Why are you always picking on me?"

When you ask her to open the door and she screams, "I'm too ugly, and I'm NEVER coming out!" believe her. She's never coming out.

*Nancy Kennedy*

## POKING AND PERSISTENCE

Cindy couldn't tell if she dreamed that her husband was shaking her shoulder or if he was really trying to awaken her. As she sleepily tried to open her eyes, she saw that he was clear over on his side of their king-sized bed. She must have been dreaming, she thought, and she groggily turned over to resume sleep. Again came the hand on her shoulder, pushing her to wakefulness. This time Cindy came fully alert and sat up in the bed.

*What is going on?* she asked herself. Occasionally she would awaken in the middle of the night and feel herself led to pray awhile before falling back to sleep, but never had she felt such an urgent pressing as now. Her heart was racing and she felt almost panicky.

"Father, what is it?" she asked. "I'm frightened. Show me clearly what's the matter with me."

Cindy had scarcely breathed the words when she saw her grandson's little face appear in her mind. Jeb was three months old, her first grandchild and healthy as he could be except for an occasional breathing problem that was controlled with nebulizer treatments, a condition that the doctors said he would outgrow. She had just talked to her son and daughter-in-law earlier in the evening and all was well except for a slight runny nose for Jeb and winter colds for the young couple.

As was her custom, she immediately prayed for the little family and settled back to sleep. But she could find no peace. It was two o'clock in the morning and she'd never had a problem getting to sleep before. She wrestled with her thoughts and continued to pray but the anxiety continued.

Finally Cindy could stand it no longer. She didn't care

what time it was; she had to know if Jeb was all right. She slipped out of bed and went to the living room to phone the kids. After four rings, their answering machine came on.

"I couldn't sleep because I felt uneasy about Jeb," she told the machine. "Please check him. I need reassurance."

Feeling she'd done the best she could she crawled back in bed only to find sleep still wouldn't come and neither would peace. Jeb's big blue eyes continued to plague her and she was increasingly nervous.

*Again came the hand on her shoulder, pushing her to wakefulness.*

Back to the telephone she went and once again reached the answering machine. She knew the young couple were heavy sleepers and their phone was located in another room so she decided to call their cell phone. Still no answer.

"This is crazy," she said to the darkness. "Why am I feeling it's so important to reach them?" She called the house phone again and left another message. Then she doggedly rang their cell phone again determined to reach a human being.

"Lord, if I'm needing to wake someone up at their house, please let it happen," she prayed. "There has to be a reason I'm bugging them in the middle of the night."

Cindy persisted in three more phone calls, alternating their house line with their cell. Finally the not-so-friendly voice of her daughter-in-law gave a sharp "hello."

"Julie, don't think I'm crazy, but I can't sleep, or the Lord won't let me sleep until someone checks on Jeb," she said. "Would it be too much to ask you to please this old grandma by taking a look-see at the baby?"

Cindy could hear Julie grumbling as she went to the nursery. The next sound she heard was a scream as the new mother shouted for her husband to come help. Then the line went dead.

Cindy paced and prayed fervently as she waited for someone to remember to call her back. "Lord, you're in this. You shook me awake. You wouldn't give me your peace. Please let me know something quickly."

Twenty minutes passed during which time Cindy awakened her husband to pray with her. Finally the phone rang and she snatched up the receiver.

"Hello, hello," she barked. "Yes, yes. Oh, thank God." Cindy explained to Julie about the night's strange events. At last, good-byes and I love yous were exchanged and Cindy sank to the sofa as she hung up the phone.

"When Julie went in Jeb's room his lips were turning blue and he was gasping for oxygen," Cindy explained to her husband. "He had so little breath that the baby monitor didn't pick up any distress sounds. They didn't call back right away because they immediately started giving him a breathing treatment and called the doctor.

"He's going to be okay, honey," she said through her tears. "They got to him in time. Thank the Lord for waking me up. Oh, thank God for his persistence."

"And thank God," her husband added as he took Cindy in his arms, "for a very stubborn grandmother."

*Vicki P. Graham*

In the supermarket was a man pushing a trolley that contained a screaming, bellowing baby. The gentleman kept repeating softly, "Don't get excited, Albert; don't scream, Albert; don't yell, Albert; keep calm, Albert."

A woman standing next to him said, "You certainly are to be commended for trying to soothe your grandson Albert."

The man looked at her and said, "Lady, I'm Albert."

*J. John and Mark Stibbe*

Having a teenage daughter is like being stuck in a hurricane. All you can do is board up your windows and look out in four years to see what the damage is.

*Buzz Nutley*

A frustrated father vented, "When I was a teenager and got in trouble, I was sent to my room without supper. But my son has his own color TV, telephone, computer and CD player in his room."

"So what do you do to him?" asked his friend.

"I send him to *my* room!" exclaimed the father.

*Jennifer Hahn*

## WHEN THE KIDS GROW UP

I was trying to find the front of my refrigerator the other day when I decided that when my kids are grown, the front of my refrigerator will be so clean I'll see myself on it. Furthermore, I won't keep a single drawing or memo there. I won't even own a refrigerator magnet.

When my kids are grown, I'll go to the mall without making three emergency trips to the bathroom.

When the kids are grown, you won't see shoes permanently planted in my living room.

I'll drive right by McDonald's and eat something nice and Chinese.

I'll go to the doctor's office and read grown-up magazines instead of *The Cat in the Hat.*

I'll walk by the most dreaded place in the grocery store and not buy any gum or mints.

I'll sit down to breakfast without people fighting over who gets the prize in the cereal box.

I'll go to the mall without going to the toy store.

I'll take a nice hot bath without removing forty-two bath toys first.

I'll leave on a business trip without worrying that the school will call and say that one of the kids is sick.

I'll wake up on a Saturday morning and bake bread, sew a skirt, or take a hike in the woods at my whim.

When the kids grow up, my husband will finish a complete sentence—maybe even a whole conversation with me—without interruption.

We'll go out to eat and get by for a small sum instead of a ransom.

I'll sit through worship services without shushing anybody or passing out pencils, gum, and offering money.

Oh, I'll suffer occasional pangs of nostalgia for all of the above—but mostly I'll miss these things as much as I now miss changing diapers in the middle of the night.

I think.

*Melodie M. Davis*

**Of all the words in all the world, I think "home" is the nicest one of all.**

*Laura Ingalls Wilder*

# 4

## Medical Mayhem

*Medicine is ever evolving and changing. We hope it's improving, but it's not perfect. So we say doctors are "practicing medicine." And while they're practicing, some pretty hilarious things happen. They can bring a smile to your face and a twinge to your funny bone.*

### MY FRIEND ACROSS THE HALL

Here we are," my stepdad, Gene, said and stopped the car. Mom sat in back, and I could feel her worried eyes on me, slumped in the passenger seat with my broken hip, busted-up leg and thirty stitches in my forehead. I looked out the window at the white-haired people sitting in their rockers on the front porch. Yeah, here I was. At Mulberry Grove, the assisted-living home where I would be staying to recuperate from my car wreck. Seemed fitting that I'd wind up with a bunch of old folks living out their last days. Not like I had much to look forward to anyway.

My girlfriend dumped me. Someone I'd trusted to help

me with my landscaping business cooked the books, and I lost my shirt and my good name. Then came the wreck. No woman, no job, no wheels . . . my life was like a bad— no, pathetic—country song.

Two aides got me into a wheelchair and pushed me onto the front porch. Every rocking chair stopped. At once, as if on cue. Heads turned to stare. I knew what they were thinking: Why in the world was a thirty-something dude moving in here? Mom and Gene came into the building behind me, loaded down with pillows, magazines, clothes and family pictures. As if any of that would help.

The aides wheeled me to my room and helped me into bed. One of them opened the blinds. Sunlight flooded in. "Close 'em," I snapped. The aide did, and they both scurried out.

Mom fussed around, hanging up my clothes, arranging pictures on the dresser. I pulled the sheet up over my head. Maybe I could just shut out Mom, the aides, this place, everything.

But a noise made me peek from under the sheet. Some old man in a wheelchair barreled into the room. Nearly took out Mom. "Youngster, welcome to my world!" he boomed. "You'll have to watch out for the girls who work here. Good-looking fellow like you. What's your name?"

I closed my eyes and kept my mouth shut.

Mom whispered, "Jeremy. Jeremy West. He's been in an accident and needs rest. You can come back later."

"He don't need rest, Mama. He needs someone to talk

to, and I'm right across the hall. Germany and I are going to be buddies."

"His name is Jeremy," Mom said tight-lipped. "J-e-r-e-m-y." In grade school my friends used to call me "Germany." Mom hated it. Funny this old codger would come up with the same nickname. I almost burst out laughing. I hadn't laughed in . . . I couldn't remember when.

"I'm Bobby Harris," the guy practically shouted. He rolled over and bumped into my bed. Might as well open my eyes. He had his gnarled hand stuck right in my face. I shook it. Good grip for an old guy.

He looked to be eighty-something. Gray hair, bifocal glasses, a short-sleeve shirt with stains I didn't want to know about and pants that, well, at one time they might have been nice. His eyes were dark brown, lively, full of

No woman, no job, no wheels . . . my life was like a bad— no, pathetic— country song.

mischief. "Germany, you and me are going to have some good times." he said, banging his cane on the floor to emphasize the point. He spit into a little cup. Tobacco-chewer to boot. Mom was so annoyed she looked ready to spit too. Bobby didn't pay her any mind. "You like the Braves, Germany? You play checkers?"

Gene kind of dragged Mom from the room. Bobby laughed and said, "Your mama thinks she's tough. She don't bother me none. I was in the army. Better be getting up, son. Almost time for lunch." He put down his spit cup and hit the call button. The aides came to get me into a wheelchair.

Like a cattle auctioneer, in the dining room Bobby announced, "This here's Germany. He's sittin' with me." Most folks looked down or away. He didn't seem to care. I suspected he liked stirring things up.

I dug into my lunch, figuring I wouldn't have to make conversation if I kept my mouth full. Surprisingly, I had an appetite, and I wolfed down everything. Bobby banged his cane and yelled, "Bring Germany some more food!" The door to the kitchen swung open and out came a server with another plate. "What about dessert?" Bobby demanded.

"Sorry. No extras today."

Bobby shoved his dessert to my side of the table. "Can't stand pineapple upside-down cake. Eat it. You hear?" What was with this guy? Couldn't he just leave me alone?

Nope. The next day Bobby called to me from the hall. "C'mon. Gospel hour in the parlor." Gospel? Yeah, right. I played asleep, but Bobby would have none of it. "Germany, son, get yourself out here," he ordered. "Ring the dang buzzer so we can get going!"

I wasn't quite sure why, but I did what Bobby said. Then, and in the days that followed. Maybe it was because I knew he wouldn't take no for an answer. Maybe it was the way he called me "son." I hadn't been called that in a long, long time, not since my father passed away when I was fifteen.

Besides, Bobby was plenty entertaining. We'd sit out on the porch after lunch and he'd start in on a story about

his time in World War II or the troublemaking he did when
he was my age, and I'd forget about how bad I felt.
Sometimes we got to laughing so hard that my stomach
hurt and Bobby had to put on his oxy-
gen gizmo. He had emphysema, but he
was in good enough shape that he'd
gotten permission to drive to his house
a couple of times a week to feed his cat.
"It's just a bit down the road," Bobby
told me. "Socks expects me." (Once
Mom heard that, her attitude toward
Bobby softened. "He can't be all bad," I
caught her whispering to Gene.)

> Maybe it was the
> way he called me
> "son." I hadn't been
> called that in a
> long, long time, not
> since my father
> passed away when I
> was fifteen.

I'd thought I would just while away
my days at Mulberry Grove lying in
bed and vegetating. Like Bobby was going to leave me any
time for that. If we weren't listening to that gospel music,
we were playing checkers. Or Bobby was teasing the nurses
and I was trying to get him to leave them be. We spent many
a night in his room drinking Cokes and watching the Atlanta
Braves on TV. He loved baseball even more than he loved
whupping me at checkers.

Before I knew it, my bones had mended enough that I
could get around with a walker. One day Mom and Gene
came to drive me to an orthopedist appointment. Bobby
charged over in his wheelchair. "Where do you think you're
taking him?" he hollered, waving his cane.

"Just to the doctor," I said.

He screwed up his face and looked . . . afraid almost. "You ain't taking him away for good, are you?"

"I'll be back in time for supper," I promised.

The light in his eyes came back on. "See ya later, Germany. Behave yourself."

The thing about Bobby was, he could never keep anything back. The day my physical therapist told me I'd always walk with a limp, Bobby bellowed, "He ain't neither. Germany ain't gonna limp through life!"

I told Bobby not to raise such a ruckus. "They'll make me leave if you keep it up."

He spit into his tobacco cup, grinned and said, "Think so?" He winked. "Me too. I need to go home and be with Socks."

His plan worked. Bobby got "dismissed." We kept in touch by phone—him talking so loud I had to hold the receiver away from my ear—but Mulberry Grove wasn't the same without him.

My doctor gave me the go-ahead to live on my own not long after that. I moved into an apartment and called Bobby to give him my new number. "Germany, son," he said, "now that you're sprung, you gotta come visit me."

The very next day Gene and Mom drove me to Bobby's. I opened the front door—he'd left it unlocked— and heard the TV blaring. Yep, he was watching the Braves, his wheelchair pulled right up to the screen. I crept up behind Bobby and hollered. He let out a yell you could hear three states away (scared poor Socks out of the room) and chewed me out big time. Then he opened his arms wide. I leaned over and gave him a hug. We talked a good long while. I noticed he was using the oxygen full-time now.

A few weeks later I got word that Bobby had died. There was a big turnout at the funeral. I made my way up to where Bobby lay in his flag-draped coffin. He wore a new black suit and a crisp white shirt. Sharp tie. I almost checked next to him for his spit cup and cane. He sure looked fine. But it was tough seeing him so still, so quiet. Peaceful, I hoped.

After the service I stood to go. My leg hurt. Felt like my heart did too. I hobbled down the aisle, holding on to the pews. Halfway to the door, something made me stop. I wasn't sure what. Then I heard Bobby talking in my head. No, hollering was more like it. *Germany, stand up straight! You ain't gonna limp through life, you hear me, son?*

I might have laughed if I hadn't been trying so hard not to cry. Strange how we'd had a chance to meet, Bobby and me, what with him being so near the end of his life. But now that I thought about it, it was I who'd been the broken-down wreck at Mulberry Grove, feeling sorry for myself, wanting to shut out the world. Until Bobby barreled in and reminded me loud and clear how much there was to live for. Baseball games on hot summer nights. Good stories. Laughter. Friendship.

I hear you, Bobby. I hear you. I stood up straight and

tall and walked out of the chapel. Slowly but steadily. No more limping through life. I was going to live—really live—every last second of it. Just like my friend Bobby.

*Jeremy West*

**There is no better surgeon than one with many scars.**

*Spanish proverb*

## 18 WAYS TO MAINTAIN A HEALTHY LEVEL OF INSANITY

1. At lunchtime, sit in your parked car with sunglasses on and point a hair dryer at passing cars. See if they slow down.

2. Page yourself over the intercom. Don't disguise your voice.

3. Every time someone asks you to do something, ask if they want fries with that.

4. Put your garbage can on your desk and label it "In."

5. Put decaf in the coffee maker for three weeks. Once everyone has gotten over their caffeine addictions, switch to espresso.

6. In the memo field of all your checks, write "for smuggling diamonds."

7. Finish all your sentences with "in accordance with the prophecy."

8. Don't use any punctuation.

9. As often as possible, skip rather than walk.

10. Order a "Diet Water" whenever you go out to eat, with a serious face.

11. Specify that your drive-through order is "to go."

12. Sing along at the opera.

13. Go to a poetry recital and ask why the poems don't rhyme.

14. Put mosquito netting around your work area and play tropical sounds all day.

15. Have your co-workers address you by your wrestling name, Rock Bottom.

16. When the money comes out of the ATM, scream "I won! I won!"

17. When leaving the zoo, start running toward the parking lot, yelling, "Run for your lives! They're loose!"

18. Tell your children over dinner, "Due to the economy, we are going to have to let one of you go."

*Author unknown*

On the way to school, the doctor had left her stethoscope on the car seat, and her little girl picked it up and began playing with it.

"Be still, my heart," thought the doctor, "my daughter wants to follow in my footsteps!" Then the child spoke into the stethoscope, "Welcome to the burger drive-thru. May I take your order?"

*Kelly John and Alie Stibbe*

Open wide and say, "Ah." What else, pray tell, could you possibly say with your mouth stretched open and a wooden stick wedged halfway down your throat?

*Mary Hollingsworth*

"HOW'S THE FAMILY?"

## SURGICAL ADVICE

I've had two tumor surgeries in my lifetime. The first one was on my thyroid.

I didn't even know I had a thyroid. I asked the doctor what it was, and he said it was right here. And then poked my throat—hard. When I'd swallow, it would move up and down.

He said, "It's got to come out, because it's probably malignant, which means you could die if you don't get it out of there. But," he added (and don't you just love those "buts"?), "I should tell you before we remove it, your laryngeal nerve runs down through there, and if I sever that nerve, you'll never make another noise." Then, he finished this nice pronouncement with a supposedly reassuring note: "Of course, I've done many of these surgeries, and I've never severed one of those nerves."

"Well," I thought, "you're probably about due, aren't you?" But what I said was, "Doctor, you sever that nerve and when I wake up, YOU'LL never make another noise."

He took the tumor out, and I remember distinctly waking up in the recovery room going, "Mi-mi-mi."

I was making NOISE. I had my nerve.

Then they found a carotid tumor on the side of my face. It's the kind that just keeps on growing until eventually I'd have another head on my shoulder. I could draw a face on it and sing a duet.

Guess what the doctor said: "Mark, your facial nerve runs down through there."

You know, there's always a nerve in the way. And guess what the doctor added.

You got it: "I should tell you before we remove it, that if I sever the nerve, the side of your face will be paralyzed."

And it would be the face I was stuck with forever. Not that I'm so great looking now, but I figured that would be worse. I could just see it. My next album cover would be *He Touched Me* with a whole new meaning.

But that story has a happy ending, too. I went through the surgery fine. In fact, I even came out with a dandy practical joke.

I learned from my first surgery that the last thing you think of before you go under the anesthesia is the first thing you think of waking up.

So listen closely, children. You can use this on your next surgery.

I planned ahead. I thought and I thought and I thought as they put me under. And when I woke up, the doctor was staring me right in the face. "Smile for me," he said.

And I did exactly what I had thought about right before I went under the gas. I did my rubber lips face contortion. You know the one. That's the face I do (my great talent) where I stretch my lips at a forty-five degree angle one way and make my mouth look like it's falling off my face the other.

And as I was stretching it as far as it would go, I said: "Mmmggmmwhat happened? Did yoummgggsever my nerve?"

Too bad I was too groggy to see the surgeon hit the floor. But I'm mighty thankful. My face today is still the perfect creation it has always been. MmggmmmSeeeee?

*Mark Lowry*

A questionnaire was sent to all the physicians in Pennsylvania concerning their favorite popular songs. The following four were the most popular as judged from the results of the questionnaire:
1. "Liver, Stay 'Way from My Door"
2. "Yes, Sir, Asthma Baby"
3. "You Take the Thyroid and I'll Take the Low Road"
4. "On a Bifocal Built for Two"

*James E. Myers*

Having a male gynecologist is like going to an auto mechanic who doesn't own a car.

*Carrie Snow*

## WORDS HOSPITAL PATIENTS DON'T WANT TO HEAR

You know what a hospital room is. It's where friends of the patient go talk to other friends of the patient. Never mind that the patient is gagging and turning blue. The visitors are going to discuss such things as the weather, taxes, the Busbee retirement pension, too much rain or the lack of it, income taxes, and "the time I had my operation."

I'll tell you, Dr. Kildare, here are a few things that, as a patient, you don't want to hear in your hospital room.

"Well, I don't think he should buy any long-playing records."

"It's a very rare disease. The only other time I've seen it is in a crossword puzzle."

"I won't tell you where we found the skin to graft on your husband's chin, but occasionally his face may feel like sitting down."

"We performed that operation just in the nick of time. Another few hours and you would have recovered without it."

"What? Three thousand dollars for an exploratory operation on my wife? Forget it, I'll find out what's wrong with her at the autopsy."

"I think my doctor used to be a veterinarian. He just told me to open my mouth and say, 'Moo.'"

"Yes, we have to operate. My malpractice premium is due tomorrow."

"Hmm, I thought they cured this years ago."

"Down at the plant, they painted out your name in the parking lot this morning."

"With this confounded new metric system, I can't

figure out this thermometer. Either he has a temperature of 415 degrees or he's going eighty-five kilometers per hour."

"If you're going to put money on today's football game, I suggest you bet only on the first half."

"I wouldn't bother watching *All in the Family* tonight. It's a two-parter."

"Of course I wear a mask when I operate. That way, they're never sure who to blame."

*And finally . . .*

Doctor: "I can't find the cause of your liver trouble, Henry. But offhand, I'd say it was due to heavy drinking."

Patient: "I understand, Doc. Why don't I just come back when you are sober?"

*Bo Whaley*

## BEDSIGHTS

It was the third day after my major back surgery. After years of moaning and groaning, I had decided the doctor was right: it was time to do something to stop the pain. I opened my eyes from a short nap, blinked, and surveyed the room. The special nurse had been dismissed, and Lawanna had gone home for a few hours to check on the girls. For the first time since being admitted to the hospital, I was on my own. I needed to get oriented because this was to be home to me for three more weeks.

The private room was small but adequate. Every square inch had been utilized. There were two chairs and a small table against the far wall on the far side of the room. A square nightstand was immediately to my right with a telephone and a nurse's call button on it. The telephone was usually just out of reach, especially for the patient recovering from surgery, and the call button kept sliding off the table to the floor.

An adjustable table on wheels had multipurpose uses. It served as a catch-all for flowers, cards and letters, pictures of family members, magazines and papers, cosmetics, electric razors, and cold water. It also functioned as a serving table for meals, so just before each meal all these items had to be stacked to make room for the tray. It took a lot of dexterity on the part of a patient to sort out all these things.

A television set was mounted high on the wall facing the bed. The bathroom, which I had not seen in three days, was about fifteen feet to my left. I would need to do a lot of picking and choosing along the obstacle course when I made that journey on my own.

In spite of the compact room I was grateful for this hospital and doctors and nurses. And I was grateful that the burning pain in the lower back would subside in a few days. Meanwhile, it was time to close my eyes again and let the pain pill do its work.

At two fifty in the afternoon the door opened and a smiling, buxom nurse asked, "And how are we doing?"

The pulsating pain spilled over into my disposition and I wanted to say, "What is there to smile about, and who is 'we'?" But an inkling of prudence restrained me. I was determined to be a good patient, especially since I was serving at the time as a trustee of the hospital.

"We need to take this to get our body functions moving again," she said as she handed me a clear plastic cup filled with chalky liquid. I knew immediately what the medicine was for and protested. And, deep down inside, I definitely resented the "we."

"Please," I begged, "I'm hurting so badly I can hardly move. I haven't done much walking since surgery, and my wife has gone home, and I have a very, very sensitive stomach. Please, I beg you, don't give me that chalky stuff. You don't understand."

"No, you need to take it. It will do you good."

I knew that any other resistance would be futile, so I took the cup with a shaky hand and downed the stuff.

> I was determined to be a good patient, especially since I was serving at the time as a trustee of the hospital.

"Thank you, Reverend McIver. We'll feel better in a little while."

I was so weary that I paid little attention to the third "we." It really didn't matter anymore. Just give me rest . . . and quiet . . . and . . .

Twenty minutes passed.

"Reverend McIver? Reverend McIver, please wake up for just a moment."

I blinked, tried to focus my eyes and mumbled, "Who? . . . What is it? . . . What time is it?"

With blurred vision, I saw another nurse standing by my bed.

"I'm Mrs. Wyrick and I'll be your nurse for this shift. It's ten minutes after three in the afternoon. Here, I have something for you."

I blinked again and saw, or thought I saw, a hint of a smile. She handed me a plastic cup filled with . . .

"Oh no! I took that stuff a few minutes ago!"

"Just swallow it, Reverend McIver. It will be good for you.

"But you don't understand! I've already had a cup of it and my back hurts, and my wife is not here, and this new brace will not let me bend . . . and . . ."

"Please, Reverend, be a good patient and just take this."

My energies were drained and my emotions depleted. The fight in me was gone. I took the plastic cup, like a "good patient," and drank the contents. Nothing seemed to matter any longer . . . except rest . . . and sleep.

Within the hour I was jarred from a deep sleep by a piercing pain in the lower abdomen. It definitely wasn't like the pain from my surgery this time! More blinding than any pain, however, was the urgency to get to the bathroom . . . immediately!

I rolled cautiously, and painfully, off the side of the bed, braced myself against the table, and stood perfectly still until the room stopped swirling. Then, groping along the walls and maneuvering around chairs, I wobbled through the obstacle course toward the bathroom. Fifteen feet seemed like fifteen miles. When I finally reached my destination, I loosened my baggy hospital pajama bottoms and watched helplessly as they fell to the floor. The pain from the low back incision, plus the rigid brace, made it nearly impossible for me to bend. But there are certain moments in life when one finds a way to do what one has to do . . . regardless!

I did. "Necessity is the mother of invention." The genius of my inventive skills really should be written up in medical journals, but I doubt that anyone but us "fellow sufferers" would appreciate them fully.

My problems were not over. Looking down I realized that I could not stoop and pick up my pajama bottoms. I leaned over as far as the pain and the brace allowed, but it wasn't far enough. I tried to grip the bottoms between my toes and lift them a few inches off the floor, but they kept slipping out of the grip. I sat there like the statue of "The Thinker," mumbling over my demise. Finally, I reached up, pulled the emergency cord, and whimpered through the speaker, "Would somebody please come to room 6228 and pull up my pajamas?"

A kind nurse responded, and helped me back to my bed.

But that was only the beginning. Again and again the pains came, and again and again I made the hazardous trek to the bathroom. After the third trip had been completed, all modesty was gone. Whatever nurse or physician or visitor happened by the room had the privilege of assisting me, whether he or she wanted to or not. Necessity is not choosy.

When ten round-trips to the bathroom had been made in less than two hours, my entire body trembled in exhaustion. Beads of perspiration dotted my forehead and I panted for breath. Even the stabbing pain in my back seemed secondary to utter and absolute fatigue. All concerns about being a good patient, an encouraging trustee or a "reverend" vanished. Enough was enough!

Weakly, I reached over and pushed the button next to my bed.

"Yes, may I help you?"

"Would you please ask Mrs. Blanton, the supervisor, to come to my room immediately?"

Two minutes later Mrs. Blanton stood at the foot of my bed. She was a tall, stately, middle-aged lady. Her hair was pulled back into a neat bun and her cap sat perfectly straight on top of her head. She was the epitome of efficiency. And she was smiling.

"How can I help you, Reverend McIver?"

"Mrs. Blanton," I began slowly and painfully, "I'm a Christian."

"Oh yes, Reverend, I know that you are a Christian." *(He's probably hallucinating.)*

"Mrs. Blanton, I'm the pastor of a church in this city."

"Yes, we all know about your wonderful church." *(I need to check his chart to see what he's been taking for pain.)*

"Mrs. Blanton," I said barely above a whisper, "I have a sensitive stomach."

"Yes?" she answered with a puzzled look. *(I have no idea what he's trying to tell me. He might have an elevated temperature.)*

"Mrs. Blanton, I tried to reason with your nurses—*two* of them! One on the previous shift and one on this shift, but they wouldn't listen." *(Goodness, he's becoming paranoid.)*

My body groaned in exhaustion, but my voice grew stronger in exasperation. "I've had two cups of some kind of chalky stuff that has driven me to the bathroom ten times in the last two hours . . . *ten times*, Mrs. Blanton!"

> All concerns about being a good patient, an encouraging trustee or a "reverend" vanished. Enough was enough!

"Well, Reverend McIver . . ."

"Ten times, Mrs. Blanton, ten . . . ten times! Everybody that has been near this room has pulled my pajama bottoms down . . . and up! . . ." *(Heavens, the "Reverend" is beginning to sound angry!)*

I paused to regain my composure and drew a deep breath. The smile on Mrs. Blanton's face was gone.

"Now," I continued slowly and deliberately and with a voice that gained momentum with every syllable, "I don't know what you have to do to stop this problem . . . and I don't care . . . but do it . . . and do it now! . . . Or . . . all hell's going to break loose on this sixth floor!"

Mrs. Blanton shot for the door with an ashen, shocked look on her face. *(Reverend McIver is becoming violent!)*

She paused as she opened the door and looked back at me in horrified astonishment.

"One other thing, Mrs. Blanton," I said with a forced smile, "don't call me 'Reverend.' I don't like the term; besides, I don't feel very 'reverent' today!"

She nodded weakly and was gone.

Three minutes later she was back with some kind of shot. I didn't ask what it was; I didn't care. Whatever she gave me worked a miracle for there were no more trips to the bathroom that day.

Before she left the hospital late that evening, Mrs. Blanton came by the room again to check on me.

"I just wanted to see how you were feeling, Rever— er . . . Pastor McIver."

"Better, thank you," I said with a grin. "By the way, what was that chalky stuff I drank twice this afternoon?"

"Haley's M.O."

"No, Mrs. Blanton, it wasn't Haley's M.O. It was Halley's Comet! And it streaked across this room all afternoon!"

She giggled nervously while struggling to maintain her professional appearance.

"I apologize for getting upset," I said quietly. "The physical pain and the emotional trauma were too much. I hope you understand."

"I understand," she responded warmly. "We all get that way at times." Then she straightened the sheets, fluffed the pillow, rearranged the cards and notes on the table, and poured me a glass of cold water. I watched as she busied herself with these tangible touches of concern. When she finished, I thanked her and she moved toward the door.

She turned the handle, paused, looked back, and said, "Sleep well tonight . . . Pastor."

We both smiled.

I'm sure I heard another smothered giggle as she closed the door.

*Bruce McIver*

My Uncle Bill had been in the hospital for several days, suffering all kinds of indignities, when my dad (his brother) came to visit. Dad knocked on the door, and Uncle Bill called out, "Friend or enema?"

*Mary Hollingsworth*

A hospital bed is a parked taxi with the meter running.

*Groucho Marx*

A hospital should also have a recovery room adjoining the cashier's office.

*Francis O. Walsh*

## INFORMATION PLEASE

A little woman called Mount Sinai Hospital. She said, "Mount Sinai Hospital? Hello. Darling, I'd like to talk with the person who gives the information about the patients. But I don't want to know if the patient is better or doing like expected or worse. I want all the information from top to bottom, from A to Z."

The voice on the other end of the line said, "Would you hold the line please? That's a very unusual request."

Then a very authoritative voice came on and said, "Are you the lady who is calling about one of the patients?"

She said, "Yes, darling! I'd like to know the information about Sarah Finkel in room 302."

He said, "Finkel. Finkel. Let me see. Feinberg, Farber— Finkel. Oh yes. Mrs. Finkel is doing very well. In fact she's had two full meals, her blood pressure is fine, and if she continues this way, her doctor is going to send her home Tuesday at twelve o'clock."

The woman said, "Thank God! That's wonderful! She's going home at twelve o'clock! I'm so happy to hear that, that's wonderful news."

The guy on the other end said, "From your enthusiasm, I take it you must be one of the close family."

She said, "What close family? I'm Sarah Finkel! My doctor don't tell me nothing!"

*Phil Stone*

I got the bill for my surgery. Now I know why those doctors were wearing masks.

*James H. Barrie*

**THE FAMILY CIRCUS**       **By Bil Keane**

"If somebody dies in the hospital, angels move them to the eternity ward."

The three stages of getting sick: ill, pill, bill.

*Bob Phillips*

## THE MIRACLE DRUGS ABROAD

Some time ago the American boss of a friend of mine told the friend, "I admire you people who live abroad. You don't take pills. In America we're always taking a pill for something or other. We're becoming a nation of hypochondriacs. But you people here don't depend on pills."

My friend agreed, "We can't get any."

Well, it was a good story, but not necessarily true. The majority of Americans coming to Europe are weighted down with every imaginable medication prescribed by family doctors. Each one is a miracle drug in its own right, and I haven't met an American tourist yet who isn't willing to share his medicines with the less fortunate people who live abroad.

Just recently I had the occasion to see how many Americans will come to the aid of their fellow man. It all started off when I complained at a dinner party of having a sore throat.

"I have just the thing for you," the hostess said. "It's Slipawhizdrene. You take one every two hours."

One of the guests said, "Slipawhizdrene is outdated. My doctor gave me Heventizeall. It doesn't make you as sleepy, and you only have to take two every four hours."

"I left the United States two weeks after you did," another woman said, "and Heventizeall has been superseded by Deviltizeall. I have a bottle at the hotel, and if you stop by I'll give you some."

The only Frenchman at the table said, "Why don't you gargle with aspirin?"

The people at the dinner couldn't have been more shocked if he had said a four-letter word. The Frenchman's American wife was so embarrassed she almost broke into tears.

He looked around helplessly. "But what did I say wrong?"

The husband of the hostess tried to smooth things over. "You see, René, in America we have gone beyond aspirin. You French believe in food; we believe in miracle drugs."

"They're all barbarians," muttered one of the Americans.

After dinner I stopped by the hotel and picked up an envelope of Deviltizeall. I took two before I went to bed. At four in the morning I no longer had my sore throat, but I was violently sick to my stomach. I had a luncheon date with a Hollywood producer, but I couldn't eat anything.

> In America we have gone beyond aspirin. You French believe in food; we believe in miracle drugs.

"I've got just the thing for an upset stomach. It's called Egazzakine. Here, take one now, and one at four o'clock."

I took the proffered pill, and in a half-hour my stomach settled. Only now, my eyes started to run, and I began sneezing.

Making my way blindly to the office, I ran into another American friend in front of the Lancaster Hotel. He recognized the symptoms immediately. "You've probably got an allergy. Come upstairs and I'll give you something for it."

We went up to his room, and he took out a leather case filled with various bottles.

"Let's see," he said, reading from a slip of paper. "The yellow-and-black ones are for jaundice, the green-and-blue ones are for pneumonia, the white-and-red ones are for rheumatism, the pink-and-beige ones are for heart trouble—oh yes, the brown-and-purple are for allergies. Here, take two now, and two at four o'clock."

"But," I protested, "I've got to take the Egazzakine at four o'clock."

"Don't do it," he warned. "That's what you're probably allergic to."

I took the brown-and-purple capsules and went to the office. In about an hour, my tear ducts had dried up and I had stopped sneezing.

I felt perfectly well, except I couldn't move my left arm.

I reported this to my friend at the Lancaster, who said, "The doctor warned me it happens sometimes. He gave me something else in case it did. I'll send it over with the bellboy."

The bellboy brought over some orange-and-cerise tablets.

I took two, and it wasn't long before I could lift my arm again.

That evening during dinner I discovered I had my sore throat back. But I didn't mention it to a soul.

*Art Buchwald*

*Virus* is a Latin word translated by doctors to mean, "Your guess is as good as mine."

*Geoff Tibbaus*

## OVERHEARD AT MY DOCTOR'S OFFICE

Excuse me, but what medical journal am I going to be in?

Do you by chance still have those pills I gave you last week? They were a string of beads my wife wanted restrung.

Yours is a common enough personality problem—you're obnoxious.

Imagine! Telling me I'm in perfect health. How does a quack like that stay in business?

Pulse, 80; temperature, 103; income, $100,000 net.

There's really nothing unusual about your condition, Mr. Hendricks, except for the fact that it is so seldom encountered in a person who is still living.

Agnes, I wish you wouldn't refer to hypodermic injections as your needlework.

Dear me, Doctor, I've been waiting so long I think I've recovered.

Take one upon going to bed and the other if you wake up in the morning.

Would you mind going to the medical convention with me this week, all expenses paid?

*Lowell D. Streiker*

(Reprinted with permission of *Medical Economics*)

**"It's that Mrs. Kasher you said was in false labor.
She wants to know how to tie that false cord."**

Three fathers paced the floor in the obstetrics waiting room. A nurse rushed in and said to one man, "Sir, you are the father of twins."

"Hey, that's great. Especially so since I'm a member of the Minnesota Twins ball team."

Soon the nurse came back and announced to the second fellow that he was the father of triplets.

"Wonderful!" exclaimed papa number two. "What a coincidence, because I'm with the 3-M Company."

The third expectant father sprang to his feet, grabbed his coat and started out. "Man, I ain't staying around here. I work for 7-Up."

*James E. Myers*

Anyone who goes to a psychiatrist should have his head examined.

*Samuel Goldwyn*

Psychiatry: the care of the id by the odd.

*Patrick Regan*

Did you hear what the white rat said to the other white rat?

"I've got that psychologist so well trained that every time I ring the bell he brings me something to eat."

*David Mercer*

Late one night in the insane asylum one inmate shouted, "I am Napoleon."

Another said, "How do you know?"

The first inmate said, "God told me."

Just then a voice from the next room shouted, "I did not."

*Bob Phillips*

## DOCTOR-SPEAK

Have you noticed that doctors' communication skills often leave something to be desired? Here are some typical examples of doctor-speak and their approximate translations.

WHAT THEY SAY:      It could be one of several things.

WHAT THEY MEAN: I haven't the foggiest idea
                what's wrong with you.

WHAT THEY SAY:      Are you sure you haven't had
                    this before?

WHAT THEY MEAN: Because you've got it again.

WHAT THEY SAY:      I'd like to run that test again.

WHAT THEY MEAN: The lab lost your blood sample.

WHAT THEY SAY:      Insurance should cover most
                    of this.

WHAT THEY MEAN: Prepare to sell your house to
                cover the rest.

WHAT THEY SAY:      These pills have very few side
                    effects.

WHAT THEY MEAN: You may experience sudden
                hair growth on your palms.

WHAT THEY SAY:      There's a lot of this going
                    around.

WHAT THEY MEAN: And we'll give it a name as soon
                as we figure out what it is.

WHAT THEY SAY:     Why don't you go over your symptoms with me one more time.

WHAT THEY MEAN: I can't remember who you are.

*Derric Johnson*

**Our doctor is an eye, ear, nose, throat, and wallet specialist.**

*Bessie and Beulah*

"WELL, WELL, LOOK WHAT WE HAVE HERE—C.R. PILLOBEE M.D.  LET'S LEAVE HIM COOLING HIS HEELS FOR AN UNREASONABLE LENGTH OF TIME."

## OL' BLUE EYES

Not long ago I was in a local bookstore, investigating one of the many new books on dieting, and discovered there was an entire diet section in the store. It was full of overweight people, lethargically pulling the volumes from the shelves and leafing through pages of information pertaining to newer and better ways to take off inches and pounds. A few were talking about that four-letter word which seems to dominate the English language—DIET.

And that isn't all. In the aisle next to the one where we were solving the problems of the avoirdupois, there were three ladies poring over a new book on exercise ... running, I believe it was. They looked fabulous. Tan. Thin. Sleek. Perfect. Yet, they confessed to one another their desire to run at least one more mile next time ... to get an even richer tan ... to work out at the club more faithfully. All of our team in the diet section were trying not to listen as they rehearsed their goals, since they, no doubt, were already outdistancing us in every way. I simply resumed munching my Almond Joy.

After locating the book I was seeking, I picked it up and started toward the cash register. On my way, I walked through an aisle labeled MENTAL HEALTH. These publications ranged from books on transcendental meditation to a volume entitled *Mental Gymnastics—Exercising While You Wait*. The person holding a copy of that appeared as though he were. His eyes were closed and I was certain he was either in a trance or not among the living, when suddenly, his eyes popped open and he realized I was looking straight at him. "Oh, I'm not doing a gymnastic," he said. "My contacts are killing me and I was trying to rest my eyes." We exchanged a few lines about the price we all pay for vanity, then we parted, the same strangers we were when we met.

On my way back to work I started thinking about all the books that must have been written on health. Countless thousands. And not only books! Good health is touted on television, radio and in films. National magazines are replete with recommended ways to be healthy and stay healthy. Of course, we all know why. Health is a treasure, and fitness is an enviable state for anyone. When we have healthy minds, bodies and spirits, we have personal assurance that we will be strong enough and sound enough to live our lives fully, coping effectively with life's problems rather than becoming the victim of them.

> Health is a treasure, and fitness is an enviable state for anyone.

But few things in life are ideal. Realistically, therefore, we must admit that the living of daily life produces all sorts of inner factions and tensions that can manifest themselves in physical pain, mental anguish, and spiritual depression. Surely, no one has trouble admitting that! That's the way things are. But . . . as we grasp good principles for healthy living, as we learn that we can prevent certain ills from occurring by simply using our heads, and as we realize that God provides marvelous promises for His children to claim and rely on when we are not well, the prognosis for a sound and healthy life becomes brighter and more probable.

However, to achieve this kind of thinking and to live on this plane, one must DO certain things to provide physical well-being, and BE certain ways to maintain the homeostasis required for one's psyche. I have hanging on the wall of my office a clever saying that reminds me of this need for balance between doing and being:

TO DO IS TO BE
—Plato
TO BE IS TO DO
—Sartre
TO DO BE DO BE DO
—Sinatra

I think "Ol' Blue Eyes" has the best outlook of all, don't you?

*Luci Swindoll*

**Laughter is the best medicine.**
*Proverbs 17:22, adapted*

# 5

## Main Street Mirth

*Towns and neighborhoods are generally about
the same: Most folks are pretty nice, but there's
always one or two . . . While the characters may
have different names, you'll probably recognize
your fellow citizens and neighbors . . . and a lot
of laughs.*

### I DO—WITH LETTUCE, ONIONS AND MUSTARD!

Hey, Preacher, there's somebody out here on the sidewalk that wants to talk to you."

What followed was like a scene from an old western
movie. Everything in Echols' Cafe came to a halt. Coffee
cups were suspended in midair; Mrs. Echols, who was pre-
siding over the cash register, rang up a bill and then forgot
to take the money; and Johnny, the cook, stopped frying
eggs and bacon and peeped through the small opening
where prepared dishes were placed. All eyes focused for a
moment on me and the table where I was having a second
cup of coffee with some ranchers. Then as if in slow motion,

the heads turned and the eyes focused through the windows on the strangers outside.

I took a last sip of coffee, pushed my chair back, 'scused myself, and walked like a man toward whatever awaited me on Main Street, Walnut Springs, Texas—population 752 people and several thousand head of cattle. Most of my buddies set their cups down, picked up their hats and followed me out the door. I knew, for I heard the shuffle of their chairs and the clomp of their boots.

Must be serious, I said to myself as I walked toward the strangers—a man and a woman. Anything's serious in Walnut Springs if it breaks up a good coffee-drinking session at Echols' Cafe on Saturday morning.

"Hi," I greeted them, "I'm the preacher." I never did like to be called *preacher*, but if they gave you a handle in this town, you lived with it.

The man said nothing; he just grinned at me. He was tall and lanky, and his hair was combed straight back and plastered down with some kind of heavy oil or cream. He was eating a hamburger. It was loaded with "the works"—meat, lettuce, onions, pickles, tomatoes and mustard. Especially mustard. Between bites he would glance down proudly at the woman beside him.

She was much shorter than he in stature, had faded brown hair that was held down by bobby pins and clips, and wore a simple, drab print dress that came nearly to her ankles. Her hands were weathered from work, the kind of work done on a farm or ranch. Lines had begun to form on her face, but behind the lines was a hint of a nervous smile. It was obvious that she was shy and embarrassed.

"What can I do for you?" I asked as people gathered around us.

The man took another bite of his burger, chewed and savored it slowly, and said, "We want to get married, and we want to know if you'll do it."

> I couldn't afford to let this stranger see the fear in my eyes.

With these words I gulped and looked down at the sidewalk. I couldn't afford to let this stranger see the fear in my eyes.

This was serious. He was asking me to marry them, and at this point as a seminary student I'd never performed a wedding ceremony. I'd only attended four weddings in my entire life. One of those was when I was four years old. Dad and I rode in his Model T Ford from Silver City, North Carolina, to Broadway where Aunt Beulah was getting married. I remember standing up and peeping over the dashboard most of the forty-mile journey, but I don't recall anything at all about the ceremony. Another wedding was my own, and I was too nervous to remember what the preacher said. I'd been to a couple of weddings of friends, but, frankly, I was more interested in decorating their cars than I was in observing the details of the service. I was a second-year seminary student, but marriage ceremonies had never been discussed in my classes.

I was in a mess—right here in the middle of Walnut Springs.

"Well," I replied with hesitation, "when would you like to get married?"

"Right now."

"Where?" I asked weakly.

"Right here's okay with us."

He grinned, took another bite of hamburger while she fidgeted awkwardly. The ranchers chuckled. They were really enjoying this.

I had to stall for time.

"I'll . . . I'll marry you," I said with as much confidence as I could muster, "but it will take a little while for me to get ready. And I don't think right here on the street is the best place. Why don't we meet at the Baptist church around the corner in forty-five minutes."

She blushed shyly and said she liked the idea, for it would give her a chance to go across the street to the variety store and purchase a new dress. He nodded his assent and I moved toward my old 1941 Chevy that was parked at an angle in front of the cafe. Pausing before I opened the door, I swallowed hard, looked back at them and waved, hoping and praying that no one would guess the uncertainties churning inside me. She didn't see my wave for she was still looking shyly at the sidewalk.

But he looked me straight in the eyes and grinned broadly. I couldn't miss the grin for his mouth was outlined perfectly with mustard!

An older friend, Cecil Macbeth, was a seasoned pastor in Meridian, twelve miles east of Walnut Springs. When I reached the house I dialed him immediately and breathed a sigh of relief when he answered the phone.

"Cecil, I need help. Quick!"

"What's wrong, Bruce?"

"There's a couple over here in Walnut Springs that wants me to marry them."

"Well, go ahead and do it."

"I can't. I don't know how."

Cecil, a soft-spoken man, calmed me down and then asked if I had a copy of the *Pastor's Manual.*

"I think so," I replied hesitantly.

"Go find it and turn to the section on weddings. You'll find a sample of a ceremony on those pages. Just read that printed ceremony at the wedding and insert the names of the persons you're marrying."

"But I don't know their names," I protested.

"Well, my friend," he chuckled, "it's time you find out. And don't forget to sign the marriage license. Good luck."

Cecil also told me that we didn't need witnesses for weddings in Texas, so just the three of us showed up at the white frame church. I was relieved for I sure didn't want any of my coffee-drinking friends watching me stumble through this situation.

She was now wearing her new dress—a light blue clinging crepe one that came to her knees. It looked exactly like something that you would buy . . . well, it looked like something you would buy at a five-and-ten-cent store.

> I was relieved for I sure didn't want any of my coffee-drinking friends watching me stumble through this situation.

He was still wearing . . . mustard, clearly outlining his broad grin.

I closed the church doors, hoping and praying that no one would wander in.

They stood before me at the front of the little church and I read the introduction like an old pro. I had penciled their names in the black manual and breezed on through the "I dos." They did—without any hesitation.

We made it through the ring ceremony, after he had dug through his pockets searching for her wedding band. I led a prayer and then pronounced them "husband and wife."

She smiled shyly. He grinned again, leaned over, and kissed her.

When they turned to thank me, I also smiled . . . for the first time . . . for both their mouths were now clearly outlined with mustard.

I headed toward home, thankful for Cecil and the *Pastor's Manual*.

As I drove slowly down Main Street, Walnut Springs, I prayed out loud, "Please, dear God, I hope she likes . . . mustard."

*Bruce McIver*

A small town is one where there is no place to go where you shouldn't.

*Alexander Woollcott*

## YOU KNOW YOU LIVE IN A
## SMALL TOWN WHEN . . .

The "road hog" in front of you on Main Street is a farmer's combine.

Second Street is on the edge of town.

You leave your jacket on the back of the chair in the cafe, and when you go back the next day, it's still there, on the same chair.

You don't signal turns because everyone knows where you're going, anyway.

No social events can be scheduled when the school gym floor is being varnished.

You call a wrong number and they supply you with the correct one.

Everyone knows all the news before it's published. They just read the hometown paper to see whether the publisher got it right.

The city limits signs are both on the same post!

The city jail is called Amoeba, because it only has one cell.

The McDonalds only has one golden arch.

The 7-11 is a 3½–5½.

The one-block-long Main Street dead-ends in both directions.

The phone book has only one page.

There's nothing doing every minute.

The ZIP code is a fraction.

Third Street is in the next town over.

A "night on the town" takes only eleven minutes.

The mayor had to annex property to eat a foot-long hot dog.

The New Year's baby was born in October.

*Author unknown*

**"Remember son, when life hands you lemons, try, try again because a penny saved gathers no moss. That pretty much covers everything."**

It was a small town, Ferguson, Ohio. When you entered there was a big sign and it said, "Welcome to Ferguson. Beware of the dog." The all-night drug-store closed at noon.

*Jackie Vernon*

## NOSTALGIA

At seven in the morning we reached Hannibal, Missouri, where my boyhood was spent . . . The only notion of the town that remained in my mind was the memory of it as I had known it when I first quitted it twenty-nine years ago. That picture of it was still as clear and vivid to me as a photograph.

I stepped ashore with the feeling of one who returns out of a dead-and-gone generation. . . . I passed through the vacant streets, still seeing the town as it was and not as it is . . . and finally climbed Holiday's Hill to get a comprehensive view. The whole town lay spread out below me then, and I could mark and fix every locality, every detail.

The things about me and before me made me feel like a boy again—convinced me that I was a boy again and that I had simply been dreaming an unusually long dream . . . From this vantage ground the extensive view up and down the river, and wide over the wooded expanses of Illinois, is very beautiful—one of the most beautiful on the Mississippi, it was satisfyingly beautiful to me . . . It had suffered no change; it was as young and fresh and comely and gracious as ever it had been; whereas, the faces of the others would be old, and scarred with the campaigns of life, and marked with their griefs and defeats, and would give me no upliftings of spirit.

During my three days' stay in the town, I woke up every morning with the impression that I was a boy—for in my dreams the faces were all young again, and looked as they had looked in the old times—but I went to bed a hundred years old, every night—for meantime I had been seeing those faces as they are now.

*Mark Twain*

We went out at 10:00 PM, did the town and went home at 10:15.

*Rusty Wright and Linda Raney Wright*

## MYSTERY

A fellow was raised in the back hills of West Virginia—I mean, so far out in the sticks, never in his life had he seen a big city, to say nothing of modern inventions and neon lights. He married a girl just like himself and they spent all their married years in the backwoods. They had one son, whom they creatively named Junior. Around the time Junior reached his sixteenth birthday, his dad began to realize it wouldn't be too many years before their son would become a man and would strike out on his own. It troubled him that his boy could reach manhood and wind up getting a job in the city, not prepared to face the real world. He felt responsible and decided to do something about it.

He and his wife started saving for a trip the three of them would take to the city. About three years later the big day arrived. They tossed their belongings in the ol' pickup and started the long journey over winding, rough roads to the city. Their plan was to spend several days at a swanky hotel and take in all the sights. As they approached the outskirts of the metropolis, Papa began to get a little jumpy: "Mama, when we pull up at th' hotel, you stay in th' truck while Junior an' I go in an' look around. We'll come back and git ya, okay?" She agreed.

Flashing neon lights and uniformed doormen greeted them as they pulled up. Mama stayed put as Papa and Junior walked wide-eyed into the lobby. Neither could believe his eyes! When they stepped on a mat, the doors opened automatically. Inside, they stood like statues, staring at the first chandelier either of them had ever seen. It hung from a ceiling three stories high. Off to the left was an enormous waterfall, rippling over inlaid stones and rocks. "Junior, look!" Papa was pointing toward a long mall where busy shoppers were going in and out of beautiful stores. "Papa, looka there!" Down below was an ice-skating rink—*inside*.

While both stood silent, watching one breathtaking sight after another, they kept hearing a clicking sound behind them. Finally, Papa turned around and saw this amazing little room with doors that slid open from the center. "What in the world?" People would walk up, push a button and wait.

Lights would flicker above the doors and then, "click," the doors would slide open from the middle. Some people would walk out of the little room and others would walk inside and turn around as, "click," the doors slid shut. By now, dad and son stood *totally* transfixed.

At that moment a wrinkled old lady shuffled up to the doors all by herself. She pushed the button and waited only a few seconds. "Click," the doors opened with a swish and she hobbled into the little room. No one else stepped in with her, so "click," the doors slid shut. Not more than twenty seconds later the doors opened again—and there stood this fabulously attractive blond, a young woman in her twenties—high heels, shapely body, beautiful face—a real knockout! As she stepped out, smiled, and turned to walk away, Papa nudged his boy and mumbled, "Hey, Junior . . . *go git Mama!*"

*Michael Green*

## YOU MIGHT BE CITY FOLK IF . . .

You don't have any problems pronouncing "Worcestershire sauce" correctly.

For breakfast, you would prefer potatoes au gratin to grits.

You don't know what a Moon Pie is.

You've never, ever, eaten okra.

You eat fried chicken with a knife and fork.

You have no idea what a polecat is.

You don't see anything wrong with putting a sweater on a poodle.

You would rather have your son become a lawyer than grow up to get his own TV fishing show.

You've never planned your summer vacation around a gun-and-knife show.

You think more money should go to important scientific research at your university than to the salary of the head football coach.

You don't have at least one can of WD-40 somewhere around the house.

The last time you smiled was when you beat someone to an on-ramp on the freeway.

You don't have any hats in your closet that advertise feed stores.

You can't spit out the car window without pulling over to the side of the road and stopping.

*Becky Freeman*

**It was such a small town we didn't even have a village idiot. We had to take turns.**

*Billy Holliday*

## DOC BRACKETT

Doc Brackett didn't have black whiskers.

Nonetheless, he was a fine man.

He doctored in our town for many years. He doctored more people than any other doctor in our town but made less money.

That was because Doc Brackett was always doctoring poor people, who had no money to pay.

He would get up in the middle of the coldest night and ride twenty miles to doctor a sick woman, or child, or to patch up some fellow who got hurt.

Everybody in our town knew Doc Brackett's office over Rice's clothing store. It was up a narrow flight of stairs. His office was always filled with people. A sign at the foot of the stairs said: DR. BRACKETT, OFFICE UPSTAIRS.

Doc Brackett was a bachelor. He was once supposed to marry Miss Elvira Cromwell, the daughter of old Junius Cromwell, the banker, but on the day the wedding was supposed to take place Doc Brackett got a call to go out into the country and doctor a Mexican child.

Miss Elvira got sore at him and called off the wedding. She said that a man who would think more of a Mexican child than of his wedding was no good. Many women in our town agreed with Miss Elvira Cromwell, but the parents of the Mexican child were very grateful to Doc Brackett when the child recovered.

For forty years, the lame, and the halt, and the blind of our town had climbed up and down the stairs to Doc Brackett's office.

He never turned anybody away.

But he lived to be seventy years old, and then one day he keeled over on the sofa in his office and died. By this time his black hair had turned white.

Doc Brackett had one of the biggest funerals ever seen in our town. Everybody went to pay their last respects when he was laid out in Gruber's undertaking parlors. He was buried in Riverview Cemetery.

There was talk of raising money to put a nice tombstone on Doc Brackett's grave as a memorial. The talk got as far as arguing about what should be carved on the stone about him. Some thought poetry would be very nice.

Doc Brackett hated poetry.

The matter dragged along and nothing whatsoever was done.

Then one day George Gruber, the undertaker, said that Doc Brackett's memorial was already over his grave, with an epitaph and all. George Gruber said the Mexican parents of the child Doc Brackett saved years ago had worried about him having no tombstone.

They had no money themselves, so they took the sign from the foot of the stairs at Doc Brackett's office and stuck it over his grave: It read: DR. BRACKETT, OFFICE UPSTAIRS.

*Damon Runyon*

### YOU MIGHT BE IN A COUNTRY CHURCH IF…

**…FINDING AND RETURNING LOST SHEEP
IS NOT JUST A PARABLE.**

David Espurvoa © Ron Birk

Billy Graham tells of a time early in his ministry when he arrived in a small town to preach. Wanting to mail a letter, he asked a young boy where the post office was. When the boy had told him, Dr. Graham thanked him and said, "If you'll come to the church this evening, you can hear me telling everyone how to get to Heaven."

"I don't think so," the boy said. "You don't even know your way to the post office."

*The World's Best Bathroom Book*

## YOU CAN'T DO THAT!

Sulphur Springs, Texas, where my parents live, has one of those famous old Texas "squares" in the middle of downtown. It's called a square because there are stores on four sides of a big open area that's as big as a city block. The open area is a huge parking lot in the center with a one-way street that goes completely around it next to the stores. It's a bit like venturing onto an English traffic roundabout, with traffic coming in at all four corners of the square, and traveling around the square until you get to the street where you need to exit. The entire area—street and parking lot—is paved with hand-laid bricks.

On the northeast corner of the square is a gorgeous, three-story, one-hundred-and-twenty-year-old courthouse made of a pinkish stone, oval windows, a domed roof, and little cupolas here and there. A truly authentic piece of Texas tradition and American nostalgia.

The square is the center of city activity. Regardless of where you're trying to go, you most always end up on the square at some point. And navigating the traffic on the square is entertaining, to say the least.

One busy Saturday morning, an old fella came into town from his place in the country to get a haircut and do his Saturday shopping. He was in an original Model T Ford, which he guided proudly into the traffic on the square. But about half way around the square, he decided he didn't want to be on the square; so he stuck his hand out the window indicating he was going to make a U-turn right in the middle of the one-way traffic.

Seeing what he was about to do, a policeman directing traffic yelled, "Hey, mister! You can't do that!"

The old man stopped, poked his head out the window, took a good look around, and yelled back, "Yeah, I think I can make it!" Then he proceeded to wind up that old Ford and drove upstream through the traffic back to the place where he'd come in and headed back to the country.

The policeman was so shocked and amused that he just let him go and stood there in the middle of the square laughing his head off.

*Clyde Shrode*

I moved recently to Cottonwood, California, a town so small it only has two streets in it—Main Street and Non-Main Street.

*Lowell D. Streiker*

A woman went into a small-town post office recently and asked for five dollars worth of stamps.

"What denomination?" asked the clerk.

"Well," came the angry reply, "I didn't know it would ever come to this. But if the nosy government people have to know, I'm a Baptist!"

*Bob Phillips*

## GETTING RID OF ANTS IS NO PICNIC

I was visiting the folks in Moreland, Georgia, and my step-father, H.B., and I walked out into the front yard.

Over near the driveway, I noticed a couple of large anthills.

"I've tried everything I know to get rid of these ants," said my stepfather. "I even put grits on them."

For a second, I thought he had said he put grits on the ants, but you'd have to be about half-addled to do something like that, and H.B. is, without doubt, of sound mind.

I know a lot about grits. I know they are misunderstood. The reason people from regions other than the South don't like grits is they have never had them prepared properly.

They are traveling through the South and stop at a HoJo for breakfast and the waitress serves them grits with their eggs and bacon.

They're probably instant grits to begin with, and I'm sure it's in the Bible somewhere that instant grits are an unholy hybrid of the real thing.

Also, our travelers don't know to put butter on their grits and then stir their eggs and bacon into them and salt and pepper to taste.

So their grits taste awful. And when they return home, they are asked, "Did you have any grits?"

And they say, "The worst thing we ever ate. Almost ruined our trip to Disney World."

But grits on an anthill?

"You didn't really put grits on these ant beds, did you?" I said to my stepfather.

"That's exactly what I said. Putting grits on ant beds is an old remedy for getting rid of ants."

"Giving Northerners unbuttered instant grits is an old remedy for getting rid of tourists, too," I said.

"What's supposed to happen," H.B. went on, "is the ants try to eat the individual little grits and they get so full they explode and die."

I've heard of other old remedies. I know if you put tobacco juice on a bee sting, it will quit hurting.

I know to put a pork chop around an ugly child's neck to get the dogs to play with him, and I know if you bury a dishrag under a full moon your warts will go away.

But, again, grits on an anthill?

So I asked, "How are the grits working on the ants?"

"These ants," answered H.B., "don't seem to be interested in grits."

"Aha!" I said. "They're Northern ants."

"How do you know?"

"Elementary," I said. "They refuse to eat grits, and look how many of them are wearing sandals with black socks."

I told my stepfather not to worry about the ants. They'd be on their way to Disney World in a matter of days.

*Lewis Grizzard*

The local orchestra was playing with great feeling, "Carry Me Back to Old Virginia." A man at a table in the corner was weeping. Touched, the leader went over to console him. "Are you a Virginian?" asked he.

"No—I'm a musician," replied the weeper.

*James Wesley Jackson*

There isn't much to be seen in a little town, but what you hear makes up for it.

*Kin Hubbard*

## MAYBE THE FRONT PORCH SHOULD COME BACK

I was driving through the outskirts of the city the other day, and I saw a man sitting on a front porch.

It was an older house and he was an older man. Modern houses don't have front porches anymore, and even if they did, younger men have far too much to do to sit on them.

I'm not certain when the front porch all but disappeared from American life, but it probably was about the same time television and air conditioning were being installed in most every home.

Why sit out on the porch where it's hot and you can get mosquito bit when you can sit inside where it's comfort-cooled and watch *Ozzie and Harriet*?

Even if an architect designs a porch today, it's usually placed in the back of the house where the hot tub is.

If we do venture out of our houses today, it's usually to get in the hot tub.

If Americans continue to spend all that time in their hot

tubs, we may all eventually shrink down like the Lilliputians and become prunelike from boiling ourselves one too many times.

I grew up in my grandparents' home. They had a front porch; we spent a lot of time sitting on it.

My grandmother would shell butter beans. My grandfather would listen for trains.

"There comes the mail train to Montgomery," he'd say, pulling his watch out of his watch pocket. "She's running four minutes late."

I learned a lot sitting on the front porch with my grandparents. How to shell butter beans. How to find the Big Dipper. How to wait for a mosquito to alight and then slap that sucker dead. What a pleasure it is to listen for trains!

Our neighbors often dropped by and sat on the porch with us.

"It was awful what happened to Norvel Tenny, wasn't it?" a neighbor would say.

"What happened to him?" my grandmother would ask, looking up from her butter beans.

"Got three fingers cut clean off down at the sawmill."

Something else I learned on the front porch—not to include sawmilling in my future.

But even my grandparents eventually moved inside. They bought a television and enclosed the front porch and made it a den.

My grandfather enjoyed westerns. My grandmother

never missed a Billy Graham sermon or a televised wrestling match. The mail train to Montgomery had to get along by itself after that.

Perhaps if front porches came back and people started sitting on them again, we'd learn to relax more and talk to one another more, and being bitten by a mosquito would at least be some contact with nature.

I probably should have stopped and talked to the old man on the porch and gotten his opinions on all of this.

I would have, too, but I was late for my tee time.

*Lewis Grizzard*

## THE CRASH OF '89

I was just plain worn out. Maybe the time had come for me to call it quits and give up my drugstore here in Cuthbert. This Southern town of ours isn't very large, just four thousand people or so. We don't even have a traffic light, just a lot of big old houses with rocking chairs on the front porches and a cluster of shops around a sleepy town square. A little south of there, across the Central of Georgia railroad tracks, Blakely Street dips to a shopping center where you'll find Central Drugs. That's the store I own— and was thinking of selling.

I've been a pharmacist since 1958, living and working in a lot of little towns not unlike Cuthbert. Five years ago I finally bought this store of my own, and my wife, Billie Jean, and I worked hard to get it on a solid footing.

When you work for yourself, you're never really off the job. Take, for instance, one Sunday not long ago: I was getting ready for church when I got a call asking me to drive into town (Billie Jean and I live about eight miles out on Old Lumpkin Road) to fill a prescription that was badly needed. No sooner had I done that and come back home when the phone rang again. Another request for another prescription, another trip back to town in my pickup. I never got to church that day. I'm not really complaining about it. After all, these are my neighbors, and it's my job, my duty, to help them. But the truth is, at the age of fifty-two I was just kind of burned out.

There was another reason for my thinking about selling the store. A big chain had offered to buy me out. It was an opportunity to make a bit of money and retire to an easier life. Here was my big chance. Should I take it?

Then came Friday night, January 13. At five minutes after closing time, I was ready to turn out the overhead fluorescent lights. The last customer in the store was waiting for me to prepare an antibiotic suspension for her sick child, but still another customer was on his way over. And I could almost be sure that the special telephone line the doctors used would be ringing any moment to tell me a patient was just leaving the office and heading my way.

I was filling the prescription behind a partition in the back of the store. Billie Jean was there too, going over some schedules with Linda, the new clerk. Out front, Candice, another salesclerk, and Jackie, our store manager, were closing up the cash register.

I looked at my watch. When was that fellow going to show up for his medicine?

The first thing I heard was Jackie yelling, really yelling. And then . . . BAM!

There was a tremendous crash. The floor shook, the walls trembled and dust came down from the ceiling. I hit the floor and covered my head. There was the sound of glass breaking, then the crunch of metal hitting metal.

And then silence.

I stood up and peered out from behind the partition. The front of the store was a mass of twisted metal, powdery rubble and shattered glass. And there, among broken bottles of mouthwash, mangled writing tablets and trembling vitamin capsules, loomed the cab of a three-quarter-ton truck. At the wheel sat the stunned customer I'd been waiting for.

No one seemed to be harmed. Billie Jean stood up, wiping dust out of her eyes. Jackie and Candice came out from behind the drug counter, where they'd leaped when they saw the truck coming. The customer was on the other side of the store, goggle-eyed but safe.

> The front of the store was a mass of twisted metal, powdery rubble and shattered glass.

I crunched through the rubble to see about the young man in the truck. There wasn't a scratch on him, but he was mighty shook up. He kept telling me how sorry he was, how his brakes had failed. Then he turned on the motor again, and with more tinkling and grinding and crashing, backed out of the store. As far as I could see, the truck had only two scrapes on it.

I couldn't say the same for Central Drugs. What moments before had been a well-stocked drugstore was now a sea of debris. Pieces of glass from the front window had been propelled thirty feet into the store. The metal shelves had been emptied of toiletries, cold remedies and stationery supplies. The smell of ammonia, hair conditioner, and nail-polish remover was overwhelming.

A cold winter wind came blasting in through the gaping hole. I went back to the pharmacy counter, where the others stood staring in stunned silence. "Call the police," I said glumly to Billie Jean. "And then call our insurance agent."

Now, almost on cue, the phone on the doctors' line started to ring. I picked up the receiver. "Doc," I said morosely, "you'd better come treat me for a heart attack. A truck just ran into my store."

I looked again at the incredible mess and just turned away. That cinched it. I was getting out of this business once and for all. My wrecked store was the last straw. Almost in a daze, I went back to finishing the antibiotic suspension I'd been working on.

A few minutes later I came out to give the customer her prescription. The police had arrived and were filling out reports with the help of that befuddled driver, whose truck was now out in the parking lot.

I was surprised to find that some friends of ours who live in town, Joan and Wendell Pearson, were in the store. Joan was at work with a broom, sweeping up the glass that had shot clear back to the pharmacy counter. They weren't the only ones, however. More people, customers I recognized, were arriving, asking to be put to work. After the crash had rattled windows blocks away and the doctor on the phone had told his patients, the word had spread throughout town.

Wendell runs Wendell's Auto and Electric, and next thing I knew, his big pickup was backed against the storefront, and folks were loading splintered paneling, twisted aluminum, broken bottles and other debris into it.

*That cinched it. I was getting out of this business once and for all.*

Candice's parents arrived. Her father, Sgt. Paul Campbell, an off-duty state trooper, organized people into teams. Someone mustered up carts and boxes, and Jackie explained to people how to sort out the jumbled mess of pencils, hair color, baby powder, and toys.

Ed Pate, a young carpenter, happened to be driving by and offered to build a temporary storefront. In no time, two carpenters and a farmer were measuring distances and laying out tools.

Charles Hardwick, the owner of True Value Hardware next door, appeared with nails and bolts, and Brook Hixon, who owned a building-supply store down the road, brought some two-by-fours and plywood.

In the meantime Wendell hauled off two truckloads of trash and was back for his third. Hammers were pounding and saws were buzzing—a sturdy frame of two-by-fours took shape where the wall and the window used to be.

I tried to count how many people were helping. At this point I think there were about eighteen—Deanne Wallace, Brenda Campbell, Ralph Bryant and Carl Rooks were just a few of them. Some people left to feed their kids but came back to do more, so I couldn't get an exact count.

There was some worry that my burglar alarm system might have been knocked out, so some of my son Robbie's friends volunteered for an all-night stakeout at the store. (It turned out that the city had a portable temporary alarm, so a stakeout wasn't necessary.)

By ten o'clock, the hole in the front of the store was covered by plywood, products were grouped back on the shelves, the floors were swept. The only mess left was a slick of hardened red fingernail polish tracked on the floor and some pieces of glass in the greeting card display, none of which would affect business the next day.

The book of Proverbs 3:28 (GNB) says, "Never tell your neighbor to wait until tomorrow if you can help him now." Well, these folks had helped me now all right. They did in four hours what would have taken our staff I don't know how long!

And so it was that the Crash of '89 knocked some sense into me. The next day I told that drugstore chain no thanks. Sure, selling out would have made a big impact on my life in terms of more money and leisure time. But it's nothing like the impact a three-quarter-ton truck—and my good neighbors in Cuthbert—made on me.

A few days ago, about ten minutes after we'd closed up for the day, a man walked up and tried the door. He didn't knock, but slowly turned to go home. I unlocked the door and called after him, "What do you need, Frank?"

"I need a prescription," he replied, "but you've been here long enough. Just go on home where you belong."

"Come on in," I said, pulling him into the store. "I am where I belong."

*Bob Buell*

A farmer was quoted in the *Town Gazette* as having "2,008 pigs." He showed up the next morning to declare to the editor, "That's a misprint! I didn't say I have 2,008 pigs. I told your reporter that I have two sows and eight pigs."

*Bob Horner*

## DELIVERING THE US MAIL

While I was in college, I worked in the campus post office. During the summer break, I landed a special student job with the post office in our town. There were three openings at the local post office, and you had to take a special kind of limited Civil Service exam to qualify. Because I had been working in the postal system for a couple of years, I had more experience than most other students. So I scored a little higher on the test than the other two applicants, and I got to do the "fun" jobs while they had to walk and carry the heavy, leather mail pouch full of mail on their shoulders eighteen miles a day. Not fun. Especially in Texas in July and August.

My job, however, was to drive an official postal truck. Each morning, the postal carriers sorted the mail for their routes, tied it into bundles arranged sequentially by addresses, and put it into mail sacks. They couldn't carry all the mail for their routes for the entire day, so relay boxes had been placed strategically around town and their sacks of mail had to be placed in those boxes. As soon as the carriers left the post office on foot, following the sequenced mail from house to house, I did what was called "running relays." That meant that I had to beat each one of the carriers to their first relay box, where they picked up their next set of mail, which led them along their routes to the next relay box. They continued this procedure all day until their sequenced mail eventually led them back to the post office.

After I ran relays, I then delivered COD's, Special Delivery letters, and the like. When I finished those jobs, I delivered parcel post to the downtown businesses. So I was running around all over town every day, not that it was very far from one side of town to the other.

In truth, I was a bit of a novelty in our small town. This was in the late 1960s, and in those days very few women worked in the postal system. If they did, they typically worked "the window," selling stamps or sorting mail into postal boxes. They were rarely seen walking a route or driving a postal truck. So people often did a double take when they saw me whizzing down the street in my red-white-and-blue Econoline van. And I took quite a bit of teasing from the mail carriers.

Every day at lunch I met my friend Emily at a burger drive-in. She was still in high school, but we had a lot of fun together.

One day we met for our ritual lunch, and while we were eating, someone tampered with the postal truck I was driving. Of course, it's a federal offense to damage a postal vehicle, punishable by a large fine or imprisonment. So when I discovered their mischief, I didn't know whether to laugh or panic.

On the side where it said "US Mail" someone had crossed out "Mail" and written "Femail."

*Mary Hollingsworth*

## HOUSE HUNTERS

Often newsletters and other regular mailings are good sources of humor. To help house hunters, *Have a Good Day* newsletter listed handy translations for real estate terms:

*Unobstructed view*: No trees.

*Waiting your imaginative touch*: Complete disrepair.

*Handyman's dream*: Owner's nightmare.

*Pond site*: Swamp, slough or marsh.

*Land alone worth purchase price*: It had better be— the house is worthless.

*House alone worth purchase price*: Small lot next to tavern.

*Central to everything*: A very noisy area.

*Easy commuting*: Remote from everything.

*Country kitchen*: No dining room.

*Charm all its own*: Don't lean on the old porch railing.

*All services available*: Nothing hooked up.

*Secluded*: No road in.

*On paved road*: House is ten feet from busy highway.

*Needs finishing touches*: Needs roof.

*Rustic appeal*: Outdoor plumbing.

*Rusty Wright and Linda Raney Wright*

A traffic safety consultant often gave talks on accident prevention. One night after he spoke to a PTA group, the program chairperson thanked him profusely and gave him a check for fifty dollars.

"Giving these presentations is a part of my job,"

the consultant said. "Could I donate the money to one of your causes?"

"That would be wonderful!" the chairperson said. "I know just the program that needs it the most. We're trying to raise money so we can afford better speakers."

*Jim Kraus*

Our town was small but we got two things we're very proud of. Night and day. If you have a year to live, move there—it'll seem like a lifetime.

*George "Goober" Lindsey*

## YOU ARE HERE

My husband, David, and I have just worked out at our neighborhood YMCA, and I am waiting for him near the men's dressing room. I have no less than a jillion things to do before the day is over, and the thought of the long day ahead fills my insides with a familiar panic. I pace up and down the hall, and when I look up, I find myself staring at a sign posted on the wall. "You are here," it says. A red arrow points to a certain location marked with an *X* on the building's blueprint.

I am still standing there looking at the sign when David comes. "This is crazy," I say to him, "but I feel so reassured knowing exactly where I am in this busy day." David laughs, puts his arm around my shoulder and off we go.

Later, I am working at my computer when the buzzer on the dryer sounds. On my way to remove David's shirts, I smell the chicken dish cooking in the kitchen and change my direction to check on it. Passing the dining room, I notice that I haven't yet set the table for tonight's guests. A moment of cold fear falls over me. *Can I really handle all of this?* Then I remember the sign. "You are here," I remind myself as I open the oven door. The casserole is fine.

After I have the shirts on hangers, I return to my desk and jot down all the things I need to accomplish before the day ends, numbering them by priority. "You are here," I say out loud as I draw a red arrow to number one on the blueprint of my day.

Realizing that today actually can be managed, one task at a time, I stop and smile. "I am here," I say to God, "and You are here. Let's turn this into a good, productive day together." And we do!

*Pam Kidd*

In the midst of a busy morning, the county agricultural agent got a call from a woman who said she was starting a chicken farm and wanted to know how long she should leave the rooster with the hens.

"Just a minute," said the agent, who was busy talking on another phone.

"Thank you very much," said the woman and hung up.

*Tal D. Bonham*

## APHORISMS FOR OUR TIME

If at first you don't succeed, skydiving is not for you.

Money can't buy happiness. But it sure makes misery easier to live with.

Vital papers will demonstrate their vitality by moving from where you left them to where you can't find them.

Always remember to pillage before you burn.

The trouble with doing something right the first time is that nobody appreciates how difficult it was.

Ray's Law: You can't fall off the floor.

Paranoids are people too; they have their own problems. It's easy to criticize, but if everybody hated you, you'd be paranoid too.

Eagles may soar, but weasels aren't sucked into jet engines.

*Jim Kraus*

When the power failed at the elementary school, the cook couldn't serve a hot meal in the cafeteria, so at the last minute she whipped up huge stacks of peanut butter and jelly sandwiches. As one little boy filled his plate, he said, "It's about time. Finally, a home-cooked meal."

*Lowell D. Streiker*

School days are the happiest days of your life—
providing, of course, your youngsters are old enough
to go.

*Paul Selden*

## HOMETOWN

The town I knew when I was small
Had nestled close beside the shore.
It wasn't very big at all—
A single street of stores and shops,
Some churches, schools, and growing crops,
Smoke curling from home chimney tops;
Such was the town I knew.

The town I knew was never rushed,
Sunrise was beautiful and bright,
Sunset was glorious and hushed.
The people were a friendly sort
Not given to unkind retort
Nor swayed by slanderous report;
Such was the town I knew.

The town I knew had two long piers
Where steamboats came across the bay,
And I can see yet through the years
A short train pull around the bend,
Stop here and there, and slowly wend
Its way to that pier journey's end;
Such was the town I knew.

The town I knew was quiet, too,
After the steamboat steamed away;
So still that I hear yet today
The rattle of a loosened plank,
A seaman's call, a chain's rude clank,
A boat's swish as it rose and sank;
Such was the town I knew.

The town I knew, today is gone;
In fifty years the tide has turned.
Self-service travel has returned,
Small pleasure craft now line the shore,
Steamboats and railroad are no more,
But in my dreams, just as before
The town I knew lives on.

*C. A. Lufburrow*

A psychiatrist was examining a country patient, a farmer who seemed not overburdened with "the smarts." He began to ask questions. "What's the opposite of sorrow?"

"Easy, Doc . . . joy."

"And the opposite of misery?"

"Even easier, Doc . . . happiness."

The physician was surprised and pleased. "You're doing great. Now tell me the opposite of woe."

"Giddyap!"

*James W. Myers*

*"Quick! Get your gun, Pa! Here come the suburbs."*

**I consider it the best part of an education to have been born and brought up in the country.**

*Louisa May Alcott*

### THE HOMETOWN

It doesn't matter much be its building great or small,
The hometown, the hometown, is the best town, after all.
The cities of the millions have the sun and stars above,
But they lack the friendly faces of the few
    you've learned to love,

And with all their pomp of riches and with all their
    teeming throngs,
The heart of man is rooted in the town where he belongs.

There are places good to visit, there are cities fair to see,
There are haunts of charm and beauty where at times it's
    good to be,
But the humblest little hamlet sings a melody to some,
And no matter where they travel it is calling them to come;
Though cities rise to greatness and are gay with gaudy dress,
There is something in the hometown which no other
    towns possess.
The hometown has a treasure which the distance
    cannot gain,
It is there the hearts are kindest, there the gentlest
    friends remain;
It is there a mystic something seems to permeate the air
To set the weary wanderer to wishing he were there;
And be it great or humble, it still holds mankind in thrall,
For the hometown, the hometown, is the best town after all.

*Edgar A. Guest*

There ain't no use talking to God when you ain't
speakin' to your neighbor.

Hambone *cartoon strip*

# 6

## Smiles over Coffee

*Friendship is the glue that holds everything together. It cements relationships between children, marriage partners, families, communities and even nations. It's life at its finest . . . and sometimes its funniest.*

### THERE'S SUCH A THING AS TOO MUCH ENCOURAGEMENT

Beth is not only a very good kidnapper, she makes a mean casserole to boot.

One day she dropped by to cheer me up. She brought with her this heavenly casserole. I mean, this casserole was amazing. It had tons of cheese and sliced eggplant and some eggs and tons of cream, and it had this Mediterranean-flavor thing happening, and it just melted in your mouth, and it was truly wonderful.

I get sort of passionate about food, if you hadn't noticed.

Anyway, so Beth shows up on my doorstep, and I make

us some coffee, and we dig into her casserole, and we spend several hours just talking about life in general and my life in particular. It was nothing short of a Kodak moment, all the encouraging and bonding and feasting that was occurring.

Early afternoon, I walked her to the door. She paused on my front porch, and our conversation began meandering toward good-byes. We chatted casually about nothing in particular, when suddenly I announced, "I'm going to make it."

Beth said, "I KNOW you're going to make it. You're strong. You're a wonderful person, and you've gone through some tough times but, yes, you're going to make it. And I'm going to be there with you every step of the way. No matter what the future holds, no matter what decisions you make with your life, I love you and I'll be there for you. You're going to be okay, Karen. This year is going to be a new chapter in your life. You're going to be fine. You really ARE going to make it."

By now there were tears in her eyes.

I blinked. I stared. Then I said, "I meant the casserole."

"The casserole?"

"I meant I'm going to make your casserole."

*Karen Scalf Linamen*

**The best mirror is an old friend.**

*George Herbert*

## WITH FRIENDS LIKE THESE

One of the most delightful weekends I had spent since moving to California six months before was nearing an end. Two teenage girls approached me while I was counting out my vitamins. "What are all those pills for?" one of them asked. "Well," I explained, "these two are for beautiful eyes, this one is for long willowy legs, that little one is for pearly white teeth . . ." and as I was waxing on, the other girl interrupted me with, "Haven't been taking them long, have you?"

*Luci Swindoll*

Sooo ... these heels are too high, huh?

## THE EMPTY EGG

He was nine, in a class of eight-year-olds. The third-graders did not welcome Philip to their group. He was *different*. He suffered from Down syndrome with all its obvious manifestations and its symptoms of retardation.

One Sunday near Easter, the Sunday school teacher poured a pile of plastic eggs that pull apart on the floor in front of the children. She told them that each child was to go outdoors during the coming week and discover some symbol of "new life" and place that symbolic seed or leaf or whatever inside the egg. Then they would open their eggs one by one, and each youngster would explain how his find was a symbol of "new life."

The children gathered around her on the appointed Sunday and put their eggs on a table, and the teacher began to open them.

One child had found a flower. All the children "oohed" and "aahed" at the lovely symbol of new life.

In another egg was a butterfly. "Beautiful," the girls said. Another was opened to reveal a rock. Some of the children laughed.

"That's crazy," one said. "How's a rock supposed to be like a new life?"

Immediately a little boy spoke up and said, "That's mine. I knew everybody would get flowers and leaves and butterflies and all that stuff, so I got a rock to be different."

Eveyone laughed. The teacher opened the last one, and there was nothing inside.

"That's not fair," someone said. "That's stupid," said another.

The teacher felt a tug on her shirt. It was Philip. Looking up he said, "It's mine. I did it. It's empty. I have new life because *the tomb is empty!*"

The class fell silent.

From that day on, Philip became part of the group. They welcomed him. Whatever had made him different was never mentioned again.

Philip's family had known he would not live a long life; just too many things were wrong with his little body. That summer, overcome with infection, Philip died.

On the day of the funeral, nine eight-year-old boys and girls confronted the reality of death and marched up to the front of the church with their Sunday school teacher. Each placed on the casket of their friend their gift of love—not flowers, but an empty plastic egg.

*Author unknown*


**Friends are God's apology for relatives.**

*Hugh Kingsmill*


**It's so much more friendly with two.**

*Piglet in* Winnie-the-Pooh *by A. A. Milne*

## A PLACE ALL TO MYSELF?

Hurrying into my dorm room, I flung my books onto the jumble of papers on my desk. One more day till Christmas break. I was looking forward to going home, but even more I relished the prospect of coming back to a room all to myself. For the whole next semester I would have no roommate! I could practically taste the freedom.

Not that I didn't like my current roomie. Third-year music students at the university, we had gotten along well. But she was moving to a house off-campus, and after the semester I would be getting married. So for the time being, I could have quiet.

I got up and walked down the hall to the bathroom. Suddenly an all-too-familiar voice called from behind: "Lisa! Lisa!"

I turned in dismay. "Hi, Megan," I said, trying to be polite. "What are you doing up here?"

"I need to talk to you." Megan was a freshman music major who had grown annoyingly fond of me. She leaned close, flashing the grin that seemed never to leave her face.

"Sure," I said, backing away. Megan was always turning up at the least-opportune time. I didn't want to dislike her, but she was too overbearing.

"I'm looking for space in your dorm next semester," she said. "Do you know anyone whose roommate might be leaving?"

"No," I said, feigning sympathy. "I don't know anyone.

I hope you find a place." I closed the bathroom door behind me.

Later that afternoon I went to the music building, where I had to make some fresh reeds for my oboe. That meant soaking a strip of new cane until it was pliant, tying it onto a cork tube, then scraping off the outer bark with a knife until it formed a reed of the right thickness that would vibrate properly. Normally I enjoyed whittling the cane. But I couldn't keep my mind on my task.

I kept thinking of Megan. Sooner or later she would find out I would be rooming by myself next semester. I hated having lied, but I couldn't bear giving up the privacy I desperately desired. And if she made me cringe during brief encounters, how would I possibly stand it day after day? Still, there had been a sense of urgency in her request that I couldn't get out of my mind.

I honed the knife on a whetstone, then scraped the reed carefully. I would be playing a solo for a holiday concert back home at my church. I needed a good reed. After pushing the cork into the top of my oboe, I put my lips against the reed and blew. Definitely too harsh. The reed was stiff.

I whittled some more, then blew again. Still not right. I tried again, but couldn't get the distinctive tone that would indicate the reed was ready. As I continued, I tried not to let my frustration and tension creep into my hands; one nick could ruin the whole reed. But the more I tried to relax, the more harried I felt.

What's wrong, Lord? Why can't I do this?

The answer became clear. I was distracted by my own lack of suppleness. Unyielding and unresponsive, the reed was producing harsh sounds instead of sweet notes. It was just like my attitude toward Megan.

"Okay, God," I said, sighing. I put down the reed, then prayed, "Forgive me for lying to Megan and for having an unloving heart toward her. I want more than anything to do your will, so if you want me to invite her to live with me, I'll do it—"

I paused. How would I be able to tell whether or not it was God's plan? I continued: "God, if you want Megan to live with me, please show me by . . . by bringing her up to this very room and having her knock on the door." That seemed safe. This was one place where Megan had never followed me—and even if she happened to pass by, she wouldn't be able to see me because the window was covered with black paper.

Nonetheless, I hedged my bets. "One more thing, God. If she shows up and knocks and then sits in the chair beside me, I'll know for sure you want me to ask her."

I was confident I had requested the impossible. The reed room was tiny and crowded. The chair next to me held a toolbox and a stack of sheet music. I had never known anyone to sit on it.

Feeling more relaxed, I returned to my work. Within an hour I finished two reeds that sounded fine. I tucked them into my velvet-lined reed case and swept string and

cane shavings into the wastebasket. It was nearing din-
nertime, Megan was clearly nowhere nearby, and I began
to visualize again the peace I would have living alone the
next semester.

There was a knock on the door.

*It can't be*, I thought. I crossed the room and opened
the door.

"Oh, you're in here," Megan said. "I was looking for
somebody else."

"I was just leaving," I said weakly.

I watched in astonishment as she edged past me,
moved the toolbox and sheet music to the table, and sat
down in the chair. "I don't quite
know what I'm doing here," she said.

I did. I was choked with surprise
at having had my prayer answered
so immediately and in such detailed
fashion. "Megan," I said, "my roommate is moving out. If you like, you
can move in with me next semester."

She threw her arms around me,
then bolted out of the room. I could
hear her running down the hall,
shouting, "I'm moving in with Lisa
next semester! Lisa said I could room with her!"

> Unyielding and
> unresponsive, the
> reed was producing
> harsh sounds
> instead of sweet
> notes. It was just
> like my attitude
> toward Megan.

After Christmas break, Megan moved in. My previous
roommate had been a casual person like me, comfortable
in clutter; Megan kept her desk and bureau orderly, which

made me attend to mine instead of letting it slip into chaos.

Living with me, Megan no longer needed to strive for my attention. She studied hard, then got to bed at a decent hour. I started adopting her schedule. Somehow my need for solitude and space didn't seem as important as the unexpected gifts of order and discipline.

We had been rooming together for four months when one night, as we were in our beds, Megan's voice came through the darkness, "Lisa? Thanks for letting me live here."

"Sure. You've been a great roommate." I meant it.

"I've never told you this, but . . ."

"But what?"

"The reason I moved out of my other dorm was because of a terrible roommate situation. A few weeks before Christmas I didn't think anyone cared about me. I was so depressed, I didn't want to live. That day I found you in the music room I was in really bad shape. Then you said I could move in with you—and that made all the difference."

I lay there marveling at the way God had brought us together, wondering which one of us had benefited more. Yes, I enjoyed a new friendship, clean room and ordered living. But I had also discovered that when God was involved in my choices, I got something far better than what I had thought I wanted.

"I'm going to miss you next year," I said. "How about

continuing on as my honorary little sister?" Even in the dark, I knew she was flashing a grin—one that had grown more appealing to me each day.

*Alisa Bair*

## FIFTEEN WAYS TO MAKE A FRIEND

Get a dog.

Exercise together.

Plan a neighborhood event.

Volunteer.

Attend a small group or women's Bible study.

Invite people to your home for dessert.

Consider attending a small fellowship rather than a megachurch.

Assume the best about people you meet.

Be interested in the details of the lives of people around you.

Use memory tricks to remember the names of people you meet.

Befriend the friendless.

Strengthen bonds with friends you already have.

Never, never, never entertain critical words or thoughts about your friends.

Be a good listener.

Don't panic during dormant times in your social life— use the time to rest, reflect or regroup.

*Karen Scalf Linamen*

## T AND D

In spite of her tiny size, she broke from her mother's womb fighting and fussing, and thankfully, perfect. Mona and Richard immediately named this long-awaited bundle of joy Tina, after Mona's mother, who had recently passed away.

Naturally, it was no surprise that she was dubbed Tiny Tina almost from the start.

Mona and Richard delighted in their big-hearted and loving little girl. Her birth followed years of prayers for a baby, but they never dreamed they'd be blessed with such a beautiful and generous child. When Tina was five, Mona and Richard put practicality aside and bought her a purebred golden retriever. The puppy's golden coat exactly matched Tina's own blond locks, and they made quite the pair as they fast became best friends. She named the puppy Sandy.

It was hard for Tina to tear herself away from her buddy to start school that year, but resolutely she marched with her mom to the school bus to begin her school career.

That afternoon, when Mona met the bus, Tina came bounding down the steps, face aglow.

"Mom, I got a new name," she yelled. "The kids like me. They gave me a new name. The kids said Tiny Tina is too hard to say, and we already have another Tina in class, so guess what my new name is?" Tina spilled out her excitement in one breath. "My name is T. See, it stands for Tina. Isn't that cool?"

Breathing a sigh of relief, Mona told her child that T was a great name and, yes, she and Dad would also call her T. Mona was sure the nickname would fade away in the next few weeks.

The name stuck. By T's third year in school, no one but teachers even recalled her real name, Mona thought ruefully. T and Sandy remained inseparable when she was out of school. The dog accompanied her, whenever possible, on visits to friends, outings, and trips to the store.

It was for a simple errand to town that Richard decided to take along T and the pet. Mona blew kisses out the kitchen window at her little family, and they waved gaily as they drove away. On the drive into town, a truck hauling concrete blocks blew a tire and swerved head-on into Richard's lane. There was nothing he could do, and he died instantly, the Highway Patrol officers assured Mona. They sadly informed her that the beautiful golden dog had been killed too.

She slumped with relief, and with dread, when the troopers told her Tina had been badly injured and was on her way to the hospital. One of the men drove her car while she rode in the patrol car to the trauma unit.

For three hours Mona paced the surgery waiting room. Thankfully, friends had joined her by then and they murmured words of encouragement and offered prayers for Tina. At last a doctor approached the little group.

"I have very good news," he smiled at Mona. "Your daughter should totally recover, except for one problem. Tina's ears were badly damaged. She will probably never hear again. She is totally deaf."

Mona collapsed into her friends' arms. She tried to focus on the good news, but all she could think was her precious T would never hear her mother's voice again, and how could she explain her daddy's and Sandy's deaths?

Somehow, Mona made it through the next few days. With her friends' help she printed a letter to Tina about the car wreck. She could tell by Tina's expression that the eight-year-old comprehended that her faithful companion and her dad were dead. She didn't know if T's body-wracking sobs were for her loss or for the knowledge she'd never hear again.

When Tina finally arrived home from the hospital, she wandered the backyard morosely. She missed her doggy. At night she cried in loneliness when no warm, snuggly animal cuddled up next to her. When the doctors told Mona that she should try to enroll Tina in a school for the hearing impaired, Mona rebelled. She knew she could handle any needs of Tina's, and she was determined not to remove her from the only school and town T had ever known.

Within weeks, however, and despite going back to school, Mona recognized the signs of depression in Tina.

"It's because she can't communicate to her friends or teachers without a lot of trouble," the school counselor told Mona. "She really needs to learn to sign, and so do you."

"But she can still talk," Mona protested, panicking at the very thought of sending her little girl away to school.

"Yes," the counselor patiently replied. "But in a few years people won't understand her as she loses her ability to correctly sound out words. Mona knew the kind counselor was right, but she refused to entertain the idea of sending Tina away to school. She stubbornly researched for answers

> She didn't know if T's body-wracking sobs were for her loss or for the knowledge she'd never hear again.

and finally found what she was looking for. A private academy for deaf children accepted day students who were not required to live on campus. The location was hundreds of miles from Mona's friends and relatives, but she resolved to make the move.

Mona thought her prayers were being answered when Tina seemed to regain her confidence at the new school. Unlike the first time, Mona was thrilled when her daughter came running in from school one day signing as fast as her little fingers would move.

"The school kids are calling me T, just like before," she spelled out. "Isn't that great? That means they like me."

"Wonderful," Mona signed back. She, along with other parents of hearing impaired children, had learned to sign quite skillfully.

But something still wasn't healed for Tina. Mona couldn't understand what was responsible for the emptiness she saw in T's eyes, the lonely look that would pass over her little face when she thought her mom wasn't watching.

The answer came suddenly one night when Mona glanced in the child's bedroom as she signed her nightly prayers.

"God, please send me another gold doggy," Tina prayed on her fingers, "one just exactly like my Sandy. Thank you."

*She misses her dog*, Mona thought. *I should have known that was the problem.*

Her thoughts were confirmed the very next day when Tina told her mom what she wanted for her approaching birthday which was coming up shortly.

"I want another golden retriever, Mommy," she said aloud. "Please, please Mama," the youngster pleaded.

Mona's heart broke, not just at the deterioration of Tina's speaking, but because her tight budget allowed no extra money for such an expensive purchase. "We'll see," Mona signed the standard adult answer for impossible requests from children. When Tina's face fell and her eyes filled with tears, Mona resolved that she would find a way to fill the void for Tina.

Every day when she arrived home from work, Mona scanned the classified ads. She called every dog breeder in the telephone directory, and there were golden retrievers, all right, to the tune of six hundred dollars a puppy. Inquiries at pet stores turned up similar reports. Attempts to persuade Tina to accept another, less-expensive breed of dog, were fruitless. Tears would flow, and Tina would tell her mother that God was surely sending her exactly what she wanted for her birthday—another Sandy.

The day before Tina's celebration found Mona on her knees. "Father, you gave us Tiny Tina, and you allowed her to survive the wreck, and I'm so thankful. Do you suppose you could shed your grace on her another time and help us find the perfect dog, one that I can afford? Do your perfect will in our lives, Father. I trust you."

> Do your perfect will in our lives, Father. I trust you.

After Tina left for school on her birthday morning, Mona received a call from a church friend. The friend had found a dog breeder who had a litter of golden retrievers ready to leave their mother. She had no idea of the price but thought Mona might be able to talk him into her price range, if she went to see him personally.

Hope filled her heart as Mona made the drive to the breeder. Sure enough, the puppies were darling and exactly the color of Tina's beloved Sandy. Mona's hopes were crushed, however, when the owner told her these pups were the same as the going price, six hundred dollars. Mona explained that it was her little girl's birthday and she wanted more than anything to replace the dog that had been killed in the car wreck along with her husband. The man was sympathetic, he told her, but he must make money on these dogs, because it was his living.

Turning quickly so he wouldn't see the tears which threatened to overwhelm her, Mona walked away sadly.

"Wait a minute," he called after her. When she turned back, he walked to the fence and picked up a puppy who had gotten separated from his littermates.

"Lady, this is a pedigreed puppy, but I'll never be able to register him, and none of my customers will want to buy him for show purposes." He cradled the little ball of gold in his arms. "If you want him, you can have him."

Mona couldn't believe her ears. There must be something terribly wrong with the puppy if the breeder couldn't find anyone who wanted him.

"What's wrong that no one wants him?" she finally dared to ask.

"He's deaf," said the breeder. "Born deaf. Do you still want him?"

"Oh yes!" Mona said through her laughter and tears. "I want him. In fact," she said, cuddling the golden puppy, "he couldn't be more perfect."

As she started toward her car with the wiggly furball, she stopped. "By the way," she asked, "does the puppy have a name?"

The man grinned. "Well, it probably sounds silly, but he loves to dig, so we just call him D."

*Vicki P. Graham*

A man can always depend on three friends: an old wife, an old dog and cash.

*Henny Youngman*

Together we stick; divided we're stuck.

*Evon Hedley*

Friends come and friends go, but a true friend sticks by you like family.

*Proverbs 18:24 MSG*

## I WILL BE A FRIEND

Jack tossed the papers on my desk—his eyebrows knit into a straight line as he glared at me.

"What's wrong?" I asked.

He jabbed a finger at the proposal. "Next time you want to change anything, ask me first," he said, turning on his heels and leaving me stewing in anger.

*How dare he treat me like that*, I thought. I had changed one long sentence and corrected grammar—something I thought I was paid to do.

It's not that I hadn't been warned. The other women, who had served in my place before me, called him names I couldn't repeat. One coworker took me aside the first day.

"He's personally responsible for two different secretaries leaving the firm," she whispered.

As the weeks went by, I grew to despise Jack. It was against everything I believed in—turn the other cheek and love your enemies. But Jack quickly slapped a verbal insult on any cheek turned his way. I prayed about it, but to be honest, I wanted to put him in his place, not love him.

One day, another of his episodes left me in tears. I stormed into his office, prepared to lose my job if needed, but not before I let the man know how I felt. I opened the door and Jack glanced up.

"What?" he said abruptly.

Suddenly I knew what I had to do. After all, he deserved it.

I sat across from him. "Jack, the way you've been treating me is wrong. I've never had anyone speak to me that way. As a professional, it's wrong, and it's wrong for me to allow it to continue," I said.

Jack snickered nervously and leaned back in his chair. I closed my eyes briefly. *God help me*, I prayed.

"I want to make you a promise. I will be a friend," I said. "I will treat you as you deserve to be treated, with respect and kindness. You deserve that," I said. "Everybody does." I slipped out of the chair and closed the door behind me.

Jack avoided me the rest of the week. Proposals, specs, and letters appeared on my desk while I was at lunch, and the corrected versions were not seen again. I brought cookies to the office one day and left a batch on Jack's desk. Another day I left a note. "Hope your day is going great," it read.

Over the next few weeks, Jack reappeared. He was reserved, but there were no other episodes. Co-workers cornered me in the break room.

"Guess you got to Jack," they said. "You must have told him off good." I shook my head.

"Jack and I are becoming friends," I said in faith. I refused to talk about him. Every time I saw Jack in the hall, I smiled at him.

> I prayed about it, but to be honest, I wanted to put him in his place, not love him.

After all, that's what friends do.

One year after our "talk," I discovered I had breast cancer. I was thirty-two, the mother of three beautiful young children, and scared. The cancer had metastasized to my lymph nodes and the statistics were not great for long-term survival. After surgery, I visited with friends and loved ones who tried to find the right words to say. No one knew what to say. Many said the wrong things. Others wept, and I tried to encourage them. I clung to hope.

The last day of my hospital stay, the door darkened and Jack stood awkwardly on the threshold. I waved him in with a smile and he walked over to my bed and, without a word, placed a bundle beside me. Inside lay several bulbs.

"Tulips," he said.

I smiled, not understanding.

He cleared his throat. "If you plant them when you get

home, they'll come up next spring." He shuffled his feet. "I just wanted you to know that I think you'll be there to see them when they come up."

Tears clouded my eyes and I reached out my hand.

"Thank you," I whispered.

Jack grasped my hand and gruffly replied, "You're welcome. You can't see it now, but next spring you'll see the colors I picked out for you." He turned and left without a word.

I have seen those red and white striped tulips push through the soil every spring for over ten years now. In fact, this September the doctor will declare me cured. I've seen my children graduate from high school and enter college.

In a moment when I prayed for just the right word, a man with very few words said all the right things.

After all, that's what friends do.

*T. Suzanne Eller*

**The language of friendship is not words but meanings.**

*Henry David Thoreau*

## IT ONLY TAKES ONE

Ever wish you could do something to change the world, but get discouraged because there's only one of you?

Well, chances are you can't change the world all by yourself, at least not all at once. But you can change it . . . one act of kindness at a time.

Consider this—it only takes . . .

. . . one compliment to make someone feel appreciated.

. . . one visit or call to end someone's loneliness.

. . . one show of trust to make someone feel trustworthy.

. . . one offer of hope to end someone's hopelessness.

. . . one request for help to make someone feel needed.

. . . one person listening to make someone feel important.

. . . one burst of laughter to make others want to join in.

. . . one outstretched hand to pull someone to safety.

. . . one person caring to make someone feel valuable.

. . . one act of forgiveness to erase someone's guilt.

. . . one hug to make someone feel huggable.

It only takes one person to change the world . . . one act of kindness at a time.

*Martha Bolton*

## JUNIOR FRIENDS

I have learned to find fun in unlikely places. Fun is a mystery. You cannot trap it like an animal; you cannot catch it like the flu. But it comes without bidding, if you are looking for it.

Recently I made a trip by plane to Michigan for the

funeral of a beloved aunt. As I boarded my return flight to California, I noticed a little girl sitting all hunched up across the aisle from me. She looked so small and so afraid. The flight attendant told me she was traveling alone.

I thought, *Oh well, the attendants will look after her.* I was busy going over the last few days . . . the funeral . . . the many people who had grown older since I had last seen them . . . It was all very depressing. I knew the five-hour flight home would be my only time to be alone with my loss. I had no intention of entertaining a little six-year-old who evidently had never been on a plane before.

As the plane took off, I noticed that she shut her eyes tightly and clenched the seat belt with bone-white knuckles. I felt something inside me want to ask her to come sit by me.

When we were safely in the air, I asked the attendant if it was all right, and she replied, "Oh yes! She has never flown before. Her parents have divorced, and she's on her way to California to live with relatives she's never even met before. Thank you for caring."

My "fun" started when the hostess came through with the complimentary beverages. Darling little Suzie with her dancing black eyes said she would have a 7-Up. I asked the hostess to put it in a fancy glass, with a cherry in it, because we were pretending we were special VIP ladies taking a super trip. Having 7-Up with a cherry in it in a fancy glass may not be your idea of fun, but to a six-year-old who had never had it that way before, it was great fun. We were off to a great start.

Our pretending went on, and I could see that I had missed so much in having all boys, never learning as a mother of a girl what little girls thought of. Suzie thought the luncheon on the plane was just like miniatureland. The tiny salt containers were a great joke. The tiny cup from the salad dressing was just for Munchkins. I had so much fun, enjoying with her child's eyes, all the goodies on our trays. We had our own special tea party. The little paper umbrella anchored in the dessert caused her to remark, "I got to see *Mary Poppins* once." I knew this was one of her most special experiences, and so we pretended that she was Mary Poppins. We kept her little umbrella, and Suzie had to learn to walk like Mary Poppins, with her toes sideways and holding the umbrella up just so. She did a great imitation!

> I noticed a little girl sitting all hunched up across the aisle from me. She looked so small and so afraid.

Just taking Suzie to the little bathroom was an experience. She couldn't figure out how things worked. She wanted to know if the soap was small because somebody had used it almost all up!

When we returned to our seats, the attendant gave us both coloring books and three crayons—blue, red and yellow. So together, we colored some puppies in the book red, made a yellow gypsy and a blue ballerina. It was fun! She had lost her fear of flying, and we looked out on the cottony sea of clouds, talking about what fun it would be to walk on the clouds, holding our Mary Poppins umbrellas, and see how far we could go.

Then it was time to land. The hours had melted away. I had been a child for a few hours, playing her game, coloring her pictures, exploring her child's mind, seeing life through the eyes of a six-year-old. I had learned so much!

I will always remember that fun day, and when I eat on an airline flight, I always think of the "Munchkin" dinner Suzie and I shared that day. She got off ahead of me when we landed, and I rushed to try to catch up with her. I saw as she was swooped up into the arms of a grandmotherly lady with twinkles in her eyes. Suzie turned to me and said, "Look, Grandma, I am Mary Poppins!" She held her little umbrella up, turned her little feet sideways, and smiled a big smile of pure joy. The grandmother thanked me for looking after her, but I was the one who was taken care of that day!

It could have been a dreary, sad trip for me, lost in my own reverie of sorrow, but instead a little girl became a diamond of love and joy for me.

When life gets so heavy for you, and you wonder how you can cope with all the load, learn to put on the garment of joy for the spirit of heaviness, and fun is included in that garment of joy. Suzie turned my desert into a decorated place of joy. Look for that joy in your life, too. Don't settle for grouchiness and sorrow: settle for joy and happiness.

*Barbara Johnson*

He is your friend who pushes you nearer to God.

*Abraham Kuyper*

### FULL CIRCLE

This is a story about me and a girl named Dorothy. We were in high school together in the little Upstate New York town of Wolcott. At the time we graduated in 1932 we didn't really know each other. But we were meant to be friends. All those years ago God could see my whole life from beginning to end, and I like to think my guardian angel set things in motion.

There wasn't much to do in Wolcott in those days. It was the Depression, and there were few jobs. People left for cities like Syracuse and Rochester. My boyfriend and I had plans to get married, but in the meantime I had an idea. "Sy," I told him, "I'm going to go back to school." The high school offered a six-month postgraduate term with all kinds of interesting courses. What's more, there was a new public bus service, and it ran right past my house. I could get to school as easy as pie!

And that's where Dorothy and I found each other. She took the bus, too, from her home in nearby South Butler. We shared an economics class, and got on right away.

From then on we chummed around. At noon hours, Dorothy would say, "Let's go shopping," and we'd head downtown. We couldn't afford to buy anything, but it was fun to window-shop and dream together. *What will our future be?* I wondered.

At the end of the school session, Dorothy had bitter-sweet news for me. "I found a job in Rochester," she said. I gave her a big hug, but I had a sense our young friendship wouldn't survive long distance.

Dorothy and I were both married the following year, and I guess our lives got too busy to stay in touch. We lost track of each other, but I never forgot my friend Dorothy. Sometimes I got out my high school yearbook just to look at the two of us.

For more than thirty years, Sy and I spent winters in Florida, going down after Christmas and staying till April. One of our two sons settled in New York, but the other moved to Florida. The Sunshine State kept calling me back too.

My health decreased as my age increased, and winters in New York were hard for me. So after I was alone in life, I bought a mobile home in Florida, near my son Paul. Still, I knew I would not be able to live on my own forever. My old body had been asking for help for a long time, but I couldn't find an assisted-living place that suited me.

One day a neighbor surprised me with a newspaper. "It's from Wolcott!" I said. "I can't believe it." She'd lived there too, and now subscribed to the hometown paper. From then on, I read the news when she was through. That's how I found my friend again—a photograph in the Wolcott paper. "It's Dorothy!" I exclaimed to my neighbor. "We used to be schoolmates."

She was celebrating her ninetieth year, just like me, and wonder of wonders, she now lived in Tarpon Springs, only miles from my son and me. The address of her assisted-living home was in the article. I wrote to her right away.

Dorothy wrote back immediately. "Come visit," she said. "What are you waiting for?" Seventy years had passed, but we were chatting like schoolgirls again. Only one thing had changed. "People call me Dot now," she said. I could get used to that.

How can I describe my joy at what happened? Paul and I made a date for lunch with her the very next week. There was Dorothy—I mean, Dot— looking lovely. This place really seemed to suit her.

> Seventy years had passed, but we were chatting like schoolgirls again.

"Can you believe us?" she asked. "We're ninety!" To me she was still as youthful as I remembered. We talked about old times and laughed so much we barely ate a bite of our lunch. Paul suggested that we look around, and take a tour of the home.

I made a down payment on a room there the next day. That, too, was meant to be. When I moved in a month later there were no vacancies.

More than a year has passed since then. Lunch and dinner with Dot are now everyday events. We play pinochle and bingo (she usually wins), and we go shopping in town, just like we used to do back in Wolcott.

"Remember so and so?" one of us will say. "Wonder

whatever happened to her?" And then we get out our old high school yearbook and leaf through the pictures. Most of all, we talk about our miracle of being together again. We've come full circle, Dot and I, a perfect circle set in motion by an angel two lifetimes ago.

*Marguerite Galloway*

## SIMPLE VS. REAL FRIENDS

A simple friend has never seen you cry.

A real friend has shoulders soggy from your tears.

A simple friend doesn't know your parents' first names.

A real friend has your parents' phone numbers in her address book.

A simple friend brings a bottle of wine to your party.

A real friend comes early to help you cook and stays late to help you clean.

A simple friend hates it when you call after he has gone to bed.

A real friend asks you why you took so long to call.

A simple friend seeks to talk with you about your problems.

A real friend seeks to help you with your problems.

A simple friend wonders about your romantic history.

A real friend could blackmail you with it.

A simple friend, when visiting, acts like a guest.

A real friend opens your refrigerator and helps himself.

A simple friend thinks the friendship is over when you have an argument.

A real friend knows that it's not a friendship until after you've had a fight.

A simple friend expects you to always be there for her.

A real friend expects to always be there for you!

*Author unknown*

**A friend loves at all times. . . .**
*Proverbs 17:17 NIV*

### THE DUET

Vicki Graham and I have been best friends since we were two years old—more than sixty years now (which neither of us can imagine!). We grew up together in Sulphur, Oklahoma, on the edge of Platt National Park. Our parents were best friends at church, and we lived across the street from each other.

Vicki and I were as different as night and day. I was a princess; she was a cowgirl. I loved to stay inside and read; she wanted to go outside and play. I liked to wear dresses; she wore boots and jeans. But there were three things we both liked: playing the piano, riding horses, and each other.

We took piano lessons from the same teacher for several years when we were in grade school. And the teacher often had us play duets for recitals and programs. We loved playing together, and it was something we continued to do for fun for many years.

Vicki stopped taking piano when she got out of grade school, but I continued taking all through high school and college, and eventually I became a music teacher, which I've now done for about forty years. Vicki went on to become editor of the local newspaper, mayor of Sulphur, a published author and a licensed counselor. But back to my story.

We also both had our own horses when we were young, and we loved to ride. We rode in parades around the area and for local events. And we spent hours and hours out exploring the creeks and forests together on our four-legged friends. Sometimes we took a picnic and stayed out the entire day together (you could do that safely in those "good old days"). This, too, was a habit we continued for several years.

About 1958, when we were in high school, Vicki accidentally got her hand caught in her horse's bridle, and when the horse yanked hard on the bridle, it pulled off half of Vicki's index finger on her left hand, leaving her with one finger that was only half as long as the others. Fortunately, she recovered well from the accident—so well, in fact, that she often forgot about having a short finger at all.

One day in 1959 we were at Vicki's house just hanging out together, as high school girls do. And we decided to see if we could still play some of the old duets we had learned in grade school. We hadn't tried to play them in several years, and we thought it would be fun to try. So we sat down side by side on the piano bench as we had done so many times before.

I sat on the left, because I played the two-handed bass part of the duet. Vicki sat on the right, because she played the top two hands on this particular song. It was a fairly upbeat piece of music and Vicki's part had a dominant two-handed run of the scales in the middle of the song, while my part was the quieter rhythmic bottom notes.

> Then she started laughing. She laughed so hard, she couldn't talk. . . .

When we came to Vicki's run, I was concentrating hard on my bass part when suddenly Vicki's part just stopped, and I glanced over to see what was wrong. Then I stopped short. No Vicki! She had fallen off the piano bench and was lying on her back on the floor with a stunned look on her face.

"What happened?" I gasped.

Then she started laughing. She laughed so hard, she couldn't talk; so she simply held up her left hand to show me her half finger. She had been so engrossed in playing the duet that she had forgotten about her short finger. About halfway through the run of her scales, her short, left index finger missed the piano key, throwing her completely off balance and onto the floor.

We laughed so hard that we never did finish the song, and we still get a kick out of remembering our notorious nineteen-and-a-half-finger duet to this day.

We're best friends for life . . . and that's the long and the short of it!

*Charlotte Greeson*

Panting and perspiring, two friends on a tandem bicycle at last got to the top of a steep hill.

"That was a stiff climb," said the first man.

"It certainly was," replied the second man. "And if I hadn't kept the brake on, we would have slid down backward."

*Bob Phillips*

## FRIENDS TO THE END

It was Sunday after church, and three of my good friends and I decided to go out to lunch. We chose an upscale restaurant in a nearby town that serves unusual, albeit pricey, Mexican food dishes—the staple of life.

As we were leaving the church building and heading out to the car, Charlotte said, "Can we stop by the grocery store so I can cash a check? I don't have any money." (This was pre-ATM, drive-through, grab-your-cash-and-run days.)

Since I'd been to the bank the day before and had plenty

of cash, and in order to save time, I said, "Oh, don't worry about it; I have money. You can just pay me back later."

We got into my car and started toward Las Colinas— an expensive suburb of Dallas—where the restaurant was located. We were having a great time laughing and telling stories when about halfway there, Paula said, "Oh no! I just remembered that I spent my last twenty dollars at the drugstore on my way to church. I had to pick up some medicine for my daughter. I think I have about thirty cents left."

Again, knowing I had extra money, I said, "Well, no problem. I'm sure I have enough to cover the three of us. Don't worry about it."

"Well, if you're sure . . ."

"Really," I said, "it's no problem. Let's just go on and you can pay me back later."

We had a wonderful lunch together, enjoying the unique South-of-the-Border cuisine and fun conversation. Being old friends, we had a lot of shared experiences that we delighted in reliving over hot sauce and blue tortilla chips. We even shared a couple of high-class desserts to top the meal off on a sweet note. As we were finishing our coffee, the waiter brought the bill.

Sher picked up the bill, looked at the total, and reached for her purse. She pulled out her wallet, looked inside, and then turned an embarrassed scarlet. "Well, you're never gonna believe this," she whispered, "but I don't have any money either."

"You're kidding, right?" I asked hopefully.

"No," she said beginning to giggle nervously. "I'm as serious as a heart attack. I have no money. I forgot to go to the bank yesterday."

"Oh, wonderful!" I said. "Well, it's nice to have such a great bunch of moochers for friends," I said teasingly.

Everyone broke out laughing. The people sitting around us looked over to see what was so funny. At the same time, my three true and faithful friends all turned and looked at me with expectant expressions. Fortunately, being the only left-brained one in the bunch, I tended to plan ahead and follow my old Girl Scout motto: "Be prepared." But even I was a little worried about whether I could cover the entire bill with the money I had.

I held out my hand and Sher gave me the bill. I knew I had exactly $80.00 in my purse. When I turned the bill over, it was $72.98. With a ten percent tip for our waiter, the total was $80.28.

I put the $80 in the folder with the bill. And Paula said, "Wait!" She took out her purse and handed me the thirty cents she had left, which put us over the top by two whole pennies. When the waiter came to take the payment, I handed him the folder.

He said, "I'll be right back with your change, ladies."

And I said, "No, please just keep the change."

At that moment, my friends and I burst out laughing, grabbed our purses, and sprinted for the door. In our wake were about twenty tables of dignified restaurant guests with shocked looks on their faces, wondering what could possibly be so funny about paying the bill in such a pricey establishment.

We, however, laughed all the way home, and even today—more than fifteen years later—my three favorite moochers and I get a great laugh out of reliving that adventure. And before we go out to eat these days, I always ask, "Does everybody . . . or anybody . . . have money?"

We celebrate being friends to the end . . . of the money!

*Mary Hollingsworth*

**She's my best friend. She thinks I'm too thin, and I think she's a natural blond.**

*Carrie Snow*

**Only your real friends will tell you when your face is dirty.**

*Sicilian Proverb*

**My coat and I live comfortably together. It has assumed all my wrinkles, does not hurt me anywhere, has molded itself to my deformities and is complacent to all my movements. I only feel its presence because it keeps me warm. Old coats and old friends are the same.**

*Victor Hugo*

If you live to be a hundred, I want to live to be a hundred minus one day, so I never have to live without you.

*Winnie-the-Pooh*

## HELLO FROM HEAVEN

When the phone rang at 11:30 PM I always knew who was calling. "Hi, Berniece," I'd say. We had a routine, Berniece and I. She was my closest friend for thirty years, and we called each other every night. I couldn't remember exactly when we met, because I felt like I had always known her. So on a night in 1990 when the phone rang at 11:30, I reached for the receiver out of habit. But I hadn't spoken to Berniece for several days. She was in intensive care.

"Roberta!" said the sweet voice on the other end. There was no question. It was my friend. She sounded well and strong. I couldn't believe my ears.

Berniece and I lived nearby and we often got together, but the phone was our way of winding down after the three-to-eleven shift at our jobs. I was a proofreader for a publishing company, and Berniece worked at the Western Electric plant. Our houses were quiet when we got home, with our families fast asleep. I got in around 11:15, fixed a cup of tea and sat by the phone. Some nights I'd call, and others I'd just wait for it to ring. "Thank God for telephones, right?" I said once. Berniece chuckled. Her job was assembling them down at the plant.

We had lots of laughs in those late-night calls. We prayed together too. Having Berniece on the phone was like having a direct line to heaven. She had a powerful faith, and she bolstered mine. Mostly we talked about our children. I had one son, but Berniece had a houseful—five children she'd embraced when she married their dad. I worried the marriage would never work out. "Love is the answer," Berniece said. "You'll see." For her, love was always the answer. Their home became one of the happiest I'd ever seen. She welcomed people at the door with a grin. "Just in time for cake," she'd say. Even with her job and the children, she made marvels in the kitchen. Many times I'd hear a knock, and it would be her daughter Tina: "Mom made too much chili. Here's some for you." Berniece knew I was crazy about her chili.

The main topic of conversation in our late-night calls continued to be our children as we struggled through their growing-up years. "Let's pray," she said one night. "God understands teenagers better than we do."

Eventually Berniece had to give up her job because her health was failing. She had diabetes, and problems with her heart. She still called to chat at 11:30, but her voice was often weak.

When she was taken to the hospital in 1990 I wasn't able to see her. I was still working, and visiting hours were limited. But Tina kept me posted. "She promises to get well," Tina told me one day. "And she sends her love." Love was always the answer for Berniece.

*Dear God, make her well again. Your love is the answer.*

A few days later, Tina called, sounding worried. "Mom's getting worse," she said. That night I was thinking of Berniece and the phone rang at 11:30. Just like old times. "Berniece!" I said. "How are you?"

"You should see this!" she said. "An angel is smiling at me. An angel dressed in magenta and gold, his wings reaching the ceiling." I couldn't find words. My friend sounded so strong and excited. "Another angel is dressed in blue. They are so beautiful! I feel so good, Roberta. I'll be home in the morning." She hung up. Angels with Berniece, how perfect. And how like Berniece to want to share the vision with her best friend.

I slept soundly and woke with joy in my heart. There was a knock at my door. It was Tina. I pulled her inside. I blurted out about Berniece's call. "It couldn't be," Tina said quietly. "Mom died in her sleep last night. Around eleven-thirty."

It couldn't be, but it was true. God had healed Berniece, and she was home, just as she'd said she would be. My phone had rung with a message from my friend, direct from heaven.

*Roberta Ley*

## COME AGAIN SOON

Your letter came today amidst magazines, circulars and bills, and my heart tripped over itself in anticipation. I purposely tucked it on the bottom of the stack, saving the best for last. When finally I came to the happy yellow envelope, I paused. I went to the kitchen and fixed myself a cup of tea, then curled up in my favorite chair on the sun porch to savor every word.

It was almost like having you there with me, for we had sat talking on that porch so often before you moved away. I could hear your voice and see your laughing brown eyes. You teased me gently as always and counseled me with your quiet wisdom. You bared your troubled soul and shared your joyful heart.

So, it was with a sigh of contentment and a sense of remorse that I came to the familiar "I love you" at the end. I sat quietly for several minutes, sipping my tea, remembering . . . wishing. Please come again soon, friend. I miss you.

*Mary Hollingsworth*

What made us friends in the long ago
when first we met?
Well, I think I know;
the best in me and the best in you
hailed each other
because they knew that
always and always
since life began
our being friends was part of God's plan.

*George Webster Douglas*

# 7

# Just Call Them Laugh Lines!

*"Aging is mind over matter—if you don't mind, it doesn't matter." And laughter is a great way to get past the minding. In some ways, of course, aging isn't so funny. But those unavoidable life changes can elicit grins to help lift the burden of growing older.*

## OLD ENOUGH OR TOO OLD?

Here are some scary thoughts: I'm old enough to have a husband going through a midlife crisis. I have friends who can't remember the day President Kennedy was shot—because they weren't even born yet. I have one friend who was only five the year I got married.

I have stray chin whiskers just like the hundred-year-old Russian peasant women in *National Geographic*.

Another frightening thing I've noticed lately is that whenever I go to Wal-Mart, I drift over to the beauty section to look at the anti-aging creams and potions, the exfoliants and the rejuvenating lotions. I haven't purchased any yet, but I want to. It's just a matter of time . . . and that scares me.

Even scarier is the growing list of things I'm too old for.

I'm too old to shop at my daughters' favorite store. The last time I shopped there I came home with a pair of overall shorts. For the record, I looked adorable in them. But the one and only time I wore them, I felt conspicuous. Like in my dreams where I'm in a public place and suddenly I realize I'm not wearing a shirt.

I'm too old for overall shorts.

I'm too old for certain words like "duh" and phrases such as "way cool." I can still say "cool" and get away with it, but "way cool" is definitely out.

I also can't call teenage boys "dudes" anymore. Not since they started calling *my* house asking for *my* daughters.

Alas, I'm too old for today's teen idols. Dylan and Brandon from *Beverly Hills 90210* are too young, yet my childhood heroes—David Cassidy, Micky Dolenz, and Bobby Sherman—are all old men.

Ernie Douglas and Opie Taylor are balding.

The Fonz is gray.

The other day I got a phone call from my friend Karen, who lives in California. Of all the things we could have talked about, we discussed the benefits of taking hormone supplements transdermally and wondered whether or not alpha hydroxy lotions can work miracles on our aging faces.

The other day the girls found my old eight-track tape deck in the garage. Laura asked, "Wow, Mom. Is that, like, an antique or something?"

I've had to explain skate keys to them. Describe platform shoes and window pane tights. Pixie haircuts and *puka* shell necklaces.

We're talking major generation gap stuff. And—like middle-age spread—it's getting wider.

They like *loud* rock music. I prefer easy-listening. Quiet. Soothing. Good ol' Barry Manilow.

They like killer roller coaster rides. I like a brisk sit on a bench where I can watch.

They can eat corn dogs and Rice Krispie marshmallow treats and drink Coca-Cola Classic right before bedtime. I consider my cup of Sanka and bran muffin living dangerously.

> They can eat corn dogs and Rice Krispie marshmallow treats and drink Coca-Cola Classic right before bedtime. I consider my cup of Sanka and bran muffin living dangerously.

They think it's fun to stay up late. Here's an observation about the concept of "late." The older one gets, the earlier "late" becomes. These days, Barry and I usually start nodding off before the girls are tucked in. In fact, they often tuck *us* in.

*His mother. He thinks I look like his mother.* I took another sip of coffee and sighed. Then I laughed. *So you look and feel your age—you're supposed to. It's not a*

*crime. Besides, hasn't God said, "Even to your old age
and gray hairs I am he, I am he who will sustain you"?*
Nancy Kennedy

"I just got a new hearing aid. It's terrific. The best
money can buy. It's really helped."
"What kind is it?"
"Three o' clock."                    *Author unknown*

## THAT'S A LAUGH

Fred Allen once said, "It's bad to suppress laughter. It
goes back down and spreads to your hips."

I don't know if he was right about the hips part, but
suppressing something that's so good for us must be
unhealthy. Laughter is good. It also puts those around us
at ease (unless we're doing it while walking down the
street alone). It eases tense moments too, like when your
beautician accidentally mixes up your hair color with her
daughter's Easter egg dye. Laughter is what gets us
through our day, whatever it holds in store for us.

In fact, there are only a few times in life when the sound
of laughter probably doesn't help the situation. For instance,
you probably don't want to hear laughter when an IRS agent
is looking over your return or when you've just asked your
boss for a raise. Laughter is not the sound you long for when
they announce your upcoming solo or when you ask your girl-

friend's parents for her hand in marriage. Personally, I'd feel a little uneasy if I heard laughter after my waitress turned in my meatloaf order, nor is it what I want to hear from my bank teller when I hand him my savings account deposit slip.

Other than the above (and maybe a few more instances), laughter is usually a welcome sound. It reminds us that no matter what else is going on in our lives, for the moment at least, everything is okay. Perhaps Will Rogers summed it up best when he said, "We're only here for a spell. Get all the good laughs you can."

*Martha Bolton*

When Barbara Bush replaced Nancy Reagan as First Lady, a *New York Post* headline proclaimed, "Goodbye, First Fashion Plate—Hello, First Grandmother." Her reaction at the time: "My mail tells me a lot of fat, white-haired, wrinkled ladies are tickled pink."

*Barbara Bush*

### SHAPING UP

Middle age is when we're too young to go on Social Security and too old to get a better job.

We can still do everything we used to do, but not until tomorrow.

It takes longer to rest than it does to get tired.

Those of us wearing bifocals step off every curb as if we're testing water in a pool.

Middle age is when you don't have to own antiques to sit on something that's fifty years old.

*Tom Mullen*

## I'M TRYING TO NUMBER MY DAYS

When I was twenty-five, I sometimes worried about what people might think of me—not just what they thought of my abilities as a broadcaster, but what they thought about, well, my socks. Or my necktie—was it too wide? Too bold? Too boring? I worried that I'd made grammatical errors. Had I used the proper metaphor? Pronounced that name correctly? Was my speech intelligible and enthusiastic, or was it dry as old toast? I was convinced it was that indelible first impression that really mattered to people.

*But I was wrong!*

When I got to be forty-five, I felt much freer to be me. I discovered that it didn't matter nearly as much what other people thought. Not that I allowed myself to be careless in areas of personal grooming or habits of speech. But at middle age, I decided people would just have to accept me as I was. If they had a problem with something I had said or done, it was their business to find a way to deal with the issue. The important thing was that people thought of me as being true to myself, not putting on airs or trying to be something I wasn't.

*But I was wrong again!*

By the time I got to be sixty-five, my perspective had completely changed again! Finally I comprehended the truth, the stark realization that for all those years, people weren't thinking of me at all!

*Al Sanders*

## METHUSELAH

Methuselah ate what he found on his plate,
    And never, as people do now,
Did he note the amount of the calorie count;
    He ate it because it was chow.
He wasn't disturbed as at dinner he sat,
    Devouring a roast or a pie,
To think it was lacking in granular fat
    Or a couple of vitamins shy.
He cheerfully chewed each species of food,
    Unmindful of troubles or fears
Lest his health might be hurt
    By some fancy dessert;
And he lived over nine hundred years.

*Author unknown*

A diplomat is a man who always remembers his wife's birthday but never remembers her age.

*Robert Frost*

## REMEMBRANCE OF THINGS PAST

It's a story about an elderly couple who were getting ready for bed one night, and she said, "Oh, I just am so hungry for ice cream, and there isn't any in the house."

And he said, "I'll get some."

She said, "You're a dear. Vanilla with chocolate sauce."

And she said, "Write it down, you'll forget."

He said, "I won't forget."

She said, "With some whipped cream on top."

And he said, "Vanilla with chocolate sauce, whipped cream on top."

And she said, "And a cherry."

And he said, "And a cherry on top."

"Well," she said, "please write it down. I know you'll forget."

He said, "I won't forget. Vanilla with chocolate sauce, whipped cream, and a cherry on top."

And away he went. By the time he got back, she was already in bed, and he handed her the paper bag. She opened it, and there was a ham sandwich. And she said, "I told you to write it down—you forgot the mustard!"

*President Ronald Reagan*

I am so old that I can remember when the Dead Sea was only sick!

*Leon Liderman*

"My memory isn't as good as my forgettery."

## WHAT DOES A GRANDMA LOOK LIKE?

I was still in my thirties when my first grandchild was born. And I have to admit, I loved hearing people say, "Why, you can't be a grandmother! You just don't look old enough."

Now that I have six grandchildren, however, people don't say that as often anymore. In fact, when I mention that I have six grandchildren, they say things like, "Oh, that's nice," or "I have eight." This tends to make me more than slightly suspicious that maybe I'm not holding my own as well as I thought I was.

And yet, let's be honest. Grandmas, along with the times, have changed. I never knew my maternal grandmother, who died when my mother was eight, but my father's mother, whom we affectionately called "Omi," was the light of my life.

Now Omi looked like a grandma. She was short, pulled her salt-and-pepper hair back into a bun at the nape of her neck, wore housedresses, aprons and black platform shoes, and never showed up at our house without a coffee tin full of home-baked butter cookies.

My mom also became a respectable-looking grandma, although in a different way from Omi. Mom was a bit taller than Omi, and her hair was much shorter. She gave up wearing housedresses when Harriet Nelson retired, she only occasionally wears aprons, and I have never seen her in platform shoes.

My youngest son, however, insists she is much more grandmotherly than I am because when he was little, he used to lean on her shoulder while she read to him. He brags about her as being "soft," but accuses me of having "bony shoulders"—obviously an automatic disqualification for a grandma position.

And I'll admit, my normal attire of blue jeans, shirts and sandals doesn't do much to promote my grandma image. But then, I suppose what all this comes down to is—just what does a grandma look like anyway?

Well, thinking about all the grandmas I have ever known, I would have to say they are short, tall, fat, skinny, blonde, brunette, gray-headed, old, young, in-between, housewives, doctors, lawyers, truck drivers, politicians, American, Asian, African, European, tough, tender, soft and even bony!

But inside, we're all the same. We have hearts that say,

"I have survived motherhood, and now I'm going to take it easy and enjoy my grandchildren. If that includes a little spoiling, well, so be it. Whatever this job calls for, I will do it well."

*Kathi Mills*

**When I was younger I could remember anything, whether it happened or not.**

*Mark Twain*

## LIVING ON EASY STREET, MEMORY LANE AND GLORY ROAD

Until I attended my thirty-year reunion, I never realized how many friends I didn't have in high school. I had many acquaintances but only a handful of friends. My best friends were in my youth group or in the band. At the reunion I visited with five people from my youth group. Two had become grandmothers at the age of forty-two. They talked about babies and diapers. I talked about Chihuahuas and carpet freshener.

None of my friends from the band came, so I had to toot my own horn. I wasn't the only one. Actually, there was not as much tooting as there was at the ten-year reunion. Twenty years ago, most of them were concerned about making a name for themselves. This time, the talk centered on the names of their kids and grandkids. One fellow was the proud parent of an eighteen-month-old son. He was also glassy-eyed and heavily sedated. Before every bite at dinner he would stare off into space and say, "Open up for the choo-choo."

I really enjoyed watching people's reactions upon seeing someone for the first time in years. There were a lot of screaming women, and just like high school, I was not the object of their screams.

One woman suffered an injury right in front of me. She tried to talk to me and broke her ankle getting off her high horse. I was also amazed at how many in my class had become bilingual. When I talked to them, their words said, "Hello, how are you?" but their eyes said, "I don't have a clue who you are."

Several of my former classmates had not changed much. I evidently have changed. I must not have been bald and overweight in high school. I got more strange looks than a sumo wrestler in a health-food store. The highlight of the reunion was taking a group photo. Unfortunately they stood me next to another bald guy right in the middle. We looked like the "one" and "three" pins at the bowling alley.

I guess everyone takes a trip down memory lane now and then. For some it is not a pleasant journey because they carry more baggage than others. For me it was a fun trip, but I don't want to move there. When I was a child, I lived on Easy Street. The older I get, the more I travel down Memory Lane but the happier I am when I return. As an adult, I truly believe I am living on Glory Road.

*Martin Babb*

It's hard to feel nostalgic when you can't remember anything!

*Author unknown*

It seems that an eighty-year-old man's golf game was hampered by poor eyesight. He could hit the ball well but he couldn't see where it went. So his doctor teamed him up with a ninety-year-old man who had perfect eyesight and was willing to go along to serve as a spotter.

The eighty-year-old man hit the first ball and asked his companion if he saw where it landed.

"Yep," said the ninety-year-old.

"Where did it go?" the eighty-year-old demanded.

The ninety-year-old replied, "I don't remember."

*Lowell D. Streiker*

## HUFFIN' WITH THE HEALTH-CLUB HOTTIES

Some people pop right out of bed each morning, anxious to go for a quick, invigorating jog. To be totally honest, I would rather clean toilets than exercise—even though it does promise a nice endorphin high for all the sweat you have to go through to get it. At my age, however, I feel I no longer have a choice in the matter. It's pretty much do or dilapidate. Which is why David and I joined a health club.

Even if we haven't always practiced healthful living, since the midseventies we have been big believers in the benefits of exercise. So when a new fitness club went up just a block from our house, we decided it was time to invest in a healthy future. The only requirements were a minor membership fee, two years slave labor and a pledge of all our home equity for security.

Our new club is not one of those wholesale workout warehouses or flab-friendly YMCAs. As luck (or providence?) would have it, it's a brand-new, state-of-the-art, full-service health facility. Professional athletes train there, along with a few other famous people (although we've never actually seen them). Even the more regular members are not your average gym club tire-kickers. They are spit-in-your-hand, let's-heave-some-weight-around kick-boxer types whose primary mission in life is to one day make the cover of *Bulging Body Beautiful* magazine.

My first trip to the club revealed that I was in deep fitness weeds. Not one woman in the whole building was above a size four, and only two percent of the population appeared to be over twenty-five. Showing up in your sorry-excuse-for-workout clothes is bad enough, but walking in a place like this packing a few extra pounds, and you're asking for self-image suicide!

Whenever I go slinking around the weight machines, pretending to know how they work, it's hard not to stare at the cute, ripped girls who fiercely focus on their muscle sculpting routines. They're such a curious marvel. How do they get that inhuman power to turn down cheesecake and pasta? Do they have any idea that their thighs never touch, even when they sit down? Where can I go to buy whatever they've got that makes a woman show up at the gym every single day, whether she wants to or not?

One elite group of primo-talented girls at this club really blows me away. Imagine this: There I am, gasping my lungs out, walking a sprightly 3.5 miles per hour on the treadmill, and to my left I see a tiny, no-fat sweetheart who is going to town on her elliptical machine—and chatting away on her cell phone. I can't think straight, much less talk straight, and here this girl is having a long, highly animated conversation (in which she seems to be doing all of the talking). Minutes later the girl on the treadmill to my right opens up a textbook and reads while running at a five-mile-an-hour pace. How is this possible? I have walked on treadmills while trying, with great effort, to scan large, full-page magazine photos, but that's about the best I can do.

> If you've ever been on a treadmill, you know it requires a certain degree of agility.

If you've ever been on a treadmill, you know it requires a certain degree of agility. Several times I have found myself going at a pretty good clip when, without warning, I suddenly clunked off the back of the machine onto the floor. People pretend not to see, but you know they have to be snickering. When its horror happens to you, all you can do is pick up your shell-shocked self and *chassé jeté* for the rotating ramp like a cowboy mounting his trick horse.

It's not that I'm uncoordinated. It's just that it's easy to ride right off the edge of one of these contraptions when your attention is locked on more important things—like breathing, watching the goings on of skinny people and squinting to read the closed captioning on the TV hanging from the ceiling.

The real kicker comes one day as I'm straining to do my squats. There I am, clinching my five-pound hand weights, when I glance up and see a petite young thing doing a long series of lunges across the floor in the aerobics room while (you guessed it) talking a mile a minute on her cell phone. I can only think of one explanation for this kind of extreme behavior: a new fitness craze called Phone-a-Coach in which unseen instructors talk people through their workout from an undisclosed location.

You're probably wondering at this point why I bother with the health club at all. How much ego-bashing can one woman take? More than once it has come to my attention that I am the largest female athlete there. This is a miserable revelation—like being dressed in a formal at the company picnic. It sometimes adds fuel to my dread of daily workouts.

But whatever the price to my ego, the club does have advantages. For example, David and I can work out together several times a week. There's a variety of equipment and classes to choose from if a particular routine gets boring. All the weight machines I'll ever need are in one place, just waiting to build the muscles that are supposed to burn all this fat and strengthen my bones. And if it's true that you become like the people you associate with, then just maybe a bit of the dedication and drive I see in the girls there will someday latch on to me.

Huffin' with the health-club hotties has been hard—okay, some days, downright depressing. I won't ever look like those girls and it's highly unlikely that I will ever become an exercise addict. But God is using the women at my health club—without their saying a word—to challenge me to better health and motivate me to want to restore the original wrapper he programmed in me. Their drive and discipline speak to me, saying, "Make better choices." "Don't give up." "Consistency will make a difference." And, "We'll see you back here tomorrow . . . but you might want to do something about that T-shirt."

*Caron Chandler Loveless*

Old folks are worth a fortune, with silver in their hair, gold in their teeth, stones in their kidneys, lead in their feet, and gas in their stomachs.

*Michael Hodgin*

## AM I DRIVING?

In Cape Coral, Florida, two elderly women were out driving in a large car; both could barely see over the dashboard. As they were cruising along they came to an intersection. The stoplight was red but they just went on through the red light. The woman in the passenger seat thought to herself, I must be losing my mind, I swear we just went through a red light.

After a few more minutes they came to another intersection and the light was red again, and again they went right through. This time Bessie in the passenger seat was almost sure that the light had been red, but was really concerned that she was mistaken. She was getting nervous and decided to pay very close attention to the road and the next intersection to see what was going on.

At the next intersection, sure enough, the light was definitely red and they went right through. She turned to the woman driving and said, "Shirley! Did you know we just ran through three red lights in a row? You could have killed us!"

Shirley turned to her and said, "Oh, am I driving?"

*Lowell D. Streiker*

At the weekly Men in Motion luncheon at Central Baptist Church in Melbourne, Florida, the speaker was talking about the importance of forgiveness. He said, "The Lord has given me the command to forgive the wrongs of others, but He has not given me the ability to forget them."

From the back of the room, an older man interrupted the speaker: "Just wait a few years!"

*Via Palmer Stiles*

"I'm getting so old that all my friends in heaven will think
I didn't make it."

## THE SPIRIT IS WILLING,
## BUT THE DENTURES ARE MISSING

Grandpa and Grandma were sitting in their porch rockers, watching the beautiful sunset and reminiscing about "the good old days," when Grandma turned to Grandpa and said, "Honey, do you remember when we first started dating and you used to just casually reach over and take my hand?"

Grandpa looked over at her, smiled, and took her aged hand in his.

With a wry little smile, Grandma pressed a little further,

"Honey, do you remember how, after we were engaged, you'd sometimes lean over and suddenly kiss me on the cheek?"

Grandpa leaned slowly toward Grandma and gave her a lingering kiss on her wrinkled cheek.

Growing bolder still, Grandma said, "Honey, do you remember how, after we were first married, you'd nibble on my ear?"

Grandpa slowly got up from his rocker and headed into the house. Alarmed, Grandma said, "Honey, where are you going?"

Grandpa replied, "To get my teeth!"

*Stan Toler*

Some jokester once said, "You know you're getting older if you find you get the same sensation from a rocking chair as you once did from a roller coaster!"

*Al Sanders*

An older man met and courted an older woman. He chose a bench in a lovely park to propose to her. In the old-fashioned style, he got on his knees in front of her and said, "I have two questions. First, will you marry me?"

"Yes, I will," she answered. "And what is your second question?"

The older gentleman replied, "Will you help me up?"

*Bernard Brunsting*

## COLOR ME GRAY

It has always amazed me that people can find something good to say about the color gray. I mean, I can actually remember sitting in high school English, reading a poem that romanticized gray fog creeping in on cat's paws. (Out of respect for the writing profession, I will leave this deranged poet nameless.) Gimme a break! I don't care how poetic you are, gray is gray, and there's nothing romantic about it.

Of course, I suppose I should be perfectly honest here and admit that I never really thought much about gray, one way or the other, until a few years ago when I looked into the mirror and . . . there it was. A gray hair. Neon gray, actually. Thicker, longer and coarser than all the dark ones, and sticking straight up in the air, taunting me like some macabre warning of things to come.

Well, my first thought upon seeing this unwelcome invader was to pull it right out. That was my second thought too, so I did. Then I wrapped it very carefully in aluminum foil and waited for my husband to come home.

"Look what I found today," I announced the moment he walked through the door.

He looked at my outstretched hand, then at me, puzzled. "Aluminum foil?" he asked.

"Not aluminum foil," I explained, lifting my hand higher so he could see the horror that lay, unbidden, in the middle of that unwrapped foil.

He looked back down at my hand, then shrugged. "I give up," he said. "Sure looks like aluminum foil to me."

Things were not going the way I'd planned. After waiting all day for him to come home so I could get a little sympathy and reassurance, all I got was a guy who'd obviously gone blind during the day and couldn't see the huge gray hair gleaming up at him.

"It's a gray hair," I cried, picking it up and holding it directly in front of his face.

"Oh," was all he said.

"It's mine," I explained.

"Oh."

"Oh?" I asked, incredulously. "That's all you can say! I've just shown you my first gray hair and all you can say is 'Oh'?"

The light seemed to dawn then as his puzzled frown turned into a mischievous grin. "Oh, now I get it," he said. "You're upset because this is your first gray hair."

(I guess we can all be glad he didn't become a psychiatrist, right?)

Anyway, he eventually figured out not only why I was upset, but also why it would not be wise to tease me about it at that particular time. And, to be fair, he did try to comfort and reassure me. But it didn't work.

Every morning I'd jump out of bed and scrutinize my head in the mirror. Nothing. No more gray hairs. *A fluke*, I decided. *That's all it was, just a fluke. I probably won't get another one for years and years and . . .*

And then one morning there were three of them.

All at once. No warning. Nothing. They just appeared out of nowhere. Sticking straight up. Gray. And I knew it was all over.

So I didn't even bother to pull them out. Instead, I got out my Bible and concordance and began looking up all the scriptures I could find about gray hair. It was awesome! By the end of the day I was just about convinced that I was happy about my three gray hairs.

Just about, but not quite. So I decided to do what any normal, intelligent, fast-approaching middle-age person would do—I colored my hair.

> There it was. A gray hair. Neon gray, actually.

For several years, in fact. Until one day not too long ago, just before it was time to color my hair again, when I looked in the mirror and realized that I liked the gray that was starting to show through. (I also realized that there were now too many gray hairs to count and/or pull out, so it was either continue to color them for the rest of my life, or accept them and grow old gracefully.)

Well, I'm happy to say that I have now stopped coloring my hair and have decided to wear my gray as a badge of courage—because, believe me, that's what it took to stop covering up the inevitable.

*Kathi Mills*

I have long thought that the aging process could be slowed down if it had to work its way through Congress.

*President George H. W. Bush*

## WISDOM FROM SENIOR CITIZENS

I started with nothing. I still have most of it.

When did my wild oats turn to prunes and All Bran?

I finally got my head together, now my body is falling apart.

All reports are in. Life is now officially unfair.

If all is not lost, where is it?

It is easier to get older than it is to get wiser.

If at first you do succeed, try not to look astonished.

The first rule of holes: if you are in one, stop digging.

I tried to get a life once, but they told me they were out of stock.

I went to school to become a wit, only got halfway though.

It was so different before everything changed.

It's not hard to meet expenses; they are everywhere.

Nostalgia isn't what it used to be.

Health is merely the slowest possible rate at which one can die.

A day without sunshine is like a day in Seattle.

I wish the buck stopped here! I could use a few.

A closed mouth gathers no feet.

It's not the pace of life that concerns me, it's the sudden stop at the end.

It's hard to make a comeback when you haven't been anywhere.

Living on Earth is expensive, but it does include a trip around the sun.

The only time the world beats a path to your door is if you're in the bathroom.

If God wanted me to touch my toes, He would have put them on my knees.

Never knock on death's door, ring the bell and run (he hates that).

*Milton Berle*

I am getting old. I'm an adult, if a reluctant one. All the signs are there. I'm starting to really enjoy cafeterias. And every now and then, when I put my britches on, I have this urge to yank 'em up over my bellybutton.

My grandfather used to walk around like that. I told him if he'd cut that little plastic thing that held his shoes together when he bought them at K-Mart, he could take bigger steps. Before he died he had his britches so high, he had to pull his zipper down to see out.

*Mark Lowry*

## GREAT FAITH

An elderly lady was well-known for her faith and for her boldness in talking about it. She would stand on her front porch and shout, "PRAISE THE LORD!"

Next door to her lived an atheist who would get so angry at her proclamations he would shout, "There ain't no Lord!"

Hard times set in on the elderly lady, and she prayed for God to send her some assistance. She stood on her porch and shouted, "PRAISE THE LORD! GOD, I NEED FOOD! I AM HAVING A HARD TIME. PLEASE, LORD, SEND ME SOME GROCERIES!"

The next morning the lady went out on her porch, noted a large bag of groceries, and shouted, "PRAISE THE LORD."

The neighbor jumped from behind a bush and said, "Aha! I told you there was no Lord. God didn't buy those groceries—I did!"

The lady started jumping up and down and clapping her hands and said, "PRAISE THE LORD! He not only sent me groceries, but He made the devil pay for them. Praise the Lord!"

*The World's Best Bathroom Book*

There is a lot to be thankful for if you take the time to look at it. For example, I'm sitting here thinking how nice it is that wrinkles don't hurt.

*Ultimate Guide to Good Clean Humor*

## WHEN I AM AN OLD COOT I WILL . . .

Wear funny hats and loud ties, flowered underwear and bright yellow suspenders. I will break all the silly, proper rules and be a kid again.

Carry my sleeping bag to doctor appointments and nap on the floor in the waiting room.

Go to the Dairy Queen and dip my dentures in the hot fudge when the waitress isn't looking.

Enroll in junior college and argue with the history teacher when she gets it wrong.

Teach my dog to fetch my neighbor's morning newspaper, but I will always return it after I have read the sports and comics.

Tell the grandkids my TV is broken so they will have to listen to my stories.

Drink cold milk from the jug and iced tea from the pitcher.

I will eat blackberries from the vine, green onions from the ground and peaches from the tree, but I will not eat liver.

Hide bananas and chocolate brownies in my sock drawer and keep a jar of peanut butter under my bed.

Carry a bucket of paint in the back of my pickup truck and create handicap parking spaces wherever I think they should be.

Dance with my wife in the kitchen and nibble her ear and make her giggle. I will write little poems for her and thank her for being a saint and a soldier.

Save a lot of money on barbers.

Refuse to grow old gracefully and will leave this world as I came in—kicking, squalling and raising a stink.

Take little trips inside my head and visit with departed friends. I will dance with angels whenever I hear the music.

*Roy English*

## LAST WORDS

Ha! They couldn't hit an elephant at this dist—

Don't unplug it; it will just take a moment to fix.

Don't worry, it's not loaded.

You can take it easy . . . that train isn't coming fast.

Gimme a match. I think my gas tank is empty.

What? Your mother is going to stay another month?

*J. John and Mark Stibbe*

When I turned sixty-five, I got an AARP card, a Medicare card and senior discount cards by the dozen. I can deal them like poker—pick a card, any card! I went to the movies in Australia, and they let me in on pensioner rates.

I remember when I was fifty-eight. We were having breakfast with a few friends. It occurred to me that Denny's gives senior discounts early, so I asked the cashier, "At what age do you give senior discounts?"

"I don't know; I'll ask!" she said. Then she yelled at the top of her voice, "Larry, at what age do we give senior discounts?"

A million eyes peered at me. Larry stuck his head out of the kitchen and looked me over. "Give it to him!" he said.

*Marvin Phillips*

Old age is like a plane flying through a storm. Once you're aboard, there's nothing you can do.

*Golda Meir*

"Every day I walk for 30 minutes, I drink 8 glasses of water, and I eat 5 fruits and vegetables... BUT I'M STILL GETTING OLDER!"

## YOU KNOW YOU'RE GROWING OLDER WHEN . . .

Your teeth and your toilet are made out of the same stuff.

You stop midway on the stairs and then can't remember if you were going up or coming down.

Your grandkids think your plain boxer shorts are funny but their multicolored Batman UndeRoos are cool.

People start calling you young: "How are you feeling today, *young* man?" You know they really mean "*old* man."

Your kids start asking you strange questions, like, "Theoretically speaking, Mom, if you *had* to go to a nursing home someday, which one do you think you would prefer?"

Everything on your body hurts, and what doesn't hurt, doesn't work.

You sit down in your rocking chair and can't get it going.

You're technologically challenged by your digital, self-winding, self-setting, expand-a-band, lighted-dial, extra-large-face Fossil watch.

People start giving you large-type books and saying, "Can you see that okay, Dad?"

Everyone talks really loud, even though your hearing is perfect.

A pretty girl walks by and your pacemaker causes the garage door to go up . . . and down . . . and up . . . and down.

You take a bite of steak, and your teeth stay stuck in it.

The airline attendant offers you coffee, tea or Milk of Magnesia.

Your best friend in the world is a box of Depends.

*Mary Hollingsworth*


**May all your wrinkles be laugh lines.**

*Beth Cope*

# 8

## Lipstick Lampoon

*Women are wonderful! Sometimes wise, sometimes witty, sometimes wild and wacky. Always fascinating and completely invaluable, women make the world go 'round. It's a lipstick lampoon!*

### CHRONIC PURSE-STUFFERS CLUB

How much does your purse weigh? Five pounds? Ten? Fifteen?

If you've decided not to purchase free weights for your home because carrying your purse provides all the strength training you need, welcome to the Chronic Purse-Stuffers Club. Anyone can join. Those of us who already belong know who we are.

We're the ones whose shoulders are three inches lower on one side. We have savings accounts designated for rotator cuff surgery.

We've ceased worrying about that old advice from our mothers. You know, to wear clean underwear in case we're ever in an accident? We only worry that while we're unconscious, some poor soul will attempt to identify us by the contents of our purses. Horrifying.

Still, for all the teasing we take, those of us who belong to the Chronic Purse-Stuffers Club are handy to have around in an emergency. Not only do we carry Kleenex, hairspray, cotton balls, plastic bandages, antacid tablets and up to one hundred dollars in loose change, we also come equipped with a flare gun, a set of hand tools, a personal flotation device and all the utensils necessary for preparing fresh game over an open fire.

I'm fairly certain I could defuse a bomb using nothing but the contents of my purse. I'm positive I could make radio contact with the Pentagon. And I could probably set a broken leg and suture a small flesh wound. It's all part of who I am, a purse-toting pack rat.

If asked to admit this minor personality quirk, would I own up to it? Of course not, and neither should any other compulsive purse-stuffer. There's a perfectly logical explanation for all this stuff we carry around.

Like those old department store receipts, dating back to 1983? Those are kindling if I'm ever stranded in a blizzard and have to build a fire on short notice. And I could spread ketchup from my foil packets onto the cello-wrapped soda crackers I've been collecting from restaurant salad bars and have quite a tasty dinner if help didn't arrive until morning.

Then I could freshen up with a few moist towelettes from the fast-food drive-through and wait for the rescue plane to arrive. It would soon spot my SOS message, outlined in the snow with bright red grocery discount stamps.

So you see, Chronic Purse-Stuffers are not unorganized. Just hyper-prepared, that's all. Don't any of you neat freaks tell me to clean out my purse—you never know when you might get hit by a bus and require first aid.

And besides, you wouldn't be foolish enough to provoke someone carrying a purse this heavy, would you?

*Renae Bottom*

## THE WORLD'S SHORTEST FAIRY TALE

Once upon a time, a girl asked a guy, "Will you marry me?" The guy said, "No!"

And the girl lived happily ever after and went shopping, dancing, camping, always had a clean house, never had to cook, and did whatever else she wanted.

The end.

*Author unknown*

Hostess: Now Jenny, when you serve the guests at dinner, be careful not to spill anything.

Jenny: Not me! I won't say a word!

*Anne Kostick*

## TEXAS WOMAN

A Texan, anticipating an upcoming wedding, told his future son-in-law that he wanted his daughter to have her great-grandmother's diamond ring. But first he wanted to have it appraised. The Texan contacted a gemologist friend who agreed to determine the ring's value. Instead of a fee, she suggested lunch at one of Houston's finer restaurants as payment.

A few days later, as the Texan and the gem expert sat sipping a glass of Chablis, he showed her the ring. She took out her jeweler's loupe, examined the diamond carefully, and handed it back.

"Wow," said a diner watching from the next table. "These Texas women are tough!"

*Jim Kraus*


## NINE REASONS WHY GOD CREATED EVE

1. God was worried that Adam would get lost in the garden and would not ask for directions.

2. God knew that one day Adam would need someone to help him find the remote.

3. God knew Adam would never go out by himself and buy a new fig leaf.

4. God knew Adam would never make a doctor's or dentist's appointment on his own.

5. God knew Adam would never remember which night to put out the rubbish.

6.  God knew Adam would never handle the responsibility of childbirth.

7.  God knew Adam would need help locating his gardening implements.

8.  God knew Adam would need someone else to blame.

9.  God finished making Adam, scratched His head and said, "I can do better than that!"

*J. John and Mark Stibbe*

## IQ TEST

One day, three men are out having a relaxing day fishing, when suddenly they catch a mermaid. After hauling the mermaid up in a net, she promises that if the men set her free, she will grant each of them a wish in return. The first man doesn't believe it, so he says, "All right, if you can really grant wishes, then double my IQ." The mermaid says, "Done," and suddenly the first man starts to flawlessly recite Shakespeare and analyze it with extreme insight.

The second man is so amazed, he looks at the mermaid and says, "Triple my IQ." The mermaid says, "Done," and the second man starts to recite solutions to mathematical problems that have been stumping all of the scientists in various fields from physics to chemistry.

The third man is so enthralled with the changes in his friends, he says to the mermaid, "Quintuple my IQ." The mermaid looks at him and says, "You know, I normally don't try to change people's minds when they make a wish, but I really wish you'd reconsider."

The man responds, "Nope, I want you to increase my IQ times five, and if you don't do it, I won't set you free."

"Please," said the mermaid, "you don't know what you're asking; it'll change your entire view on the universe. Won't you ask for something else, a million dollars, anything."

But no matter what the mermaid said, the third man insisted on having his IQ increased by five times its usual power. So the mermaid finally relented and said, "Done." The third man became a woman.

*Aaron Cohl*

## HOW WOMEN SEE THEMSELVES

**Age 8**  Looks at herself and sees:
Cinderella/Sleeping Beauty.

**Age 15**  Looks at herself and sees:
Cinderella/Sleeping Beauty/Cheerleader or if she is
PMS'ing, sees: Pimples/UGLY ("Mom, I can't go to
school looking like this!")

**Age 20**  Looks at herself and sees:
"Too fat/too thin, too short/too tall, too straight/
too curly" but decides she's going out anyway.

**Age 30**  Look at herself and sees:
"Too fat/too thin, too short/too tall, too straight/
too curly" but decides she doesn't have time to fix
it so she's going out anyway.

**Age 40**  Looks at herself and sees:
"Too fat/too thin, too short/too tall, too straight/
too curly" but says, "At least, I'm clean" and goes out
anyway.

**Age 50**  Looks at herself and sees:
"I am" and goes wherever she wants to.

**Age 60**  Looks at herself and reminds herself of all the
people who can't even see themselves in the mirror
anymore and goes out and conquers the world.

**Age 70** Looks at herself and sees:
Wisdom, laughter, and ability and goes out and enjoys life.

**Age 80** Doesn't bother to look. Just puts on a red hat and goes out to participate in the world.

**Age 90** Can't see and doesn't worry about it!

*Author unknown*

## ATTITUDE

There once was a woman who woke up one morning, looked in the mirror and noticed she had only three hairs on her head.

"Well," she said, "I think I'll braid my hair today." So she did and she had a wonderful day.

The next day she woke up, looked in the mirror and saw that she had only two hairs on her head.

"Hmm," she said, "I think I'll part my hair down the middle today." So she did and she had a grand day.

The next day she woke up, looked in the mirror and noticed that she had only one hair on her head.

"Well," she said, "today I'm going to wear my hair in a pony tail." So she did and she had a fun, fun day.

The next day she woke up, looked in the mirror and noticed that there wasn't a single hair on her head.

"YEAH!" she exclaimed, "I don't have to fix my hair today!"

Attitude is everything.

*Author unknown*

## MUSIC TO SNORE BY

For many years our church chorus presented a huge musical drama centered around the resurrection of Christ. We worked on it for about six months, beginning in the fall and presented it three or four times over the weekend before Easter. Thousands of people came to see the program and celebrate with us.

The musical was a major production, including professional stage lighting, sound engineers, building stages, costuming, publishing programs, advertising and myriad other details that had to be managed. (It makes me tired just remembering it!) We loved doing it and considered it our gift to the community, our congregation, and God.

One of the first things we did to prepare for the musical was to plan a retreat for the chorus where we spent two full days learning the music. Most often we held the retreat at a Christian encampment a few miles away from our city where we wouldn't be distracted. The encampment was a wonderful place out in the open, but the amenities were few.

Our sleeping quarters, for instance, were in a huge two-sided dormitory—one side for the men, and the other side for the women. Each side was basically equipped with hard-as-rock bunk beds, concrete floors, and a bathroom with three showers and two sinks. (Now imagine twenty-five women all trying to get dressed at the same time!)

I always dreaded bedtime at these retreats because I'm

a light sleeper and any kind of noise wakes me up. With twenty-five women in the same room, you can just bet that there's always some kind of noise going on. So I generally got very little sleep and spent the next day trying to stay awake through our rehearsals.

At one retreat, the noise level was especially high, since two of our women singers snored like freight trains. Now, men snore and wear it as a badge of honor. But women do *not* like to snore or be known as snorers; it's just not considered a flattering thing to do. So it's pretty touchy when you comment on your friend's nightly noises. Telling them they sound like the Southern Pacific Railroad coming into the station is simply not a good idea.

Instead, we women try every other method we can think of to make our friends stop the obnoxious snoring *without actually waking them up*. We clear our throats, flop over in the bed so the springs rattle, cough, sneeze, wheeze, and try a variety of other sneaky little attention getters that will hopefully arouse them from the sleep of the dead. Usually all that happens is that we succeed in waking ourselves up even more, and the snorer continues sawing logs without interruption.

On this particular night, the noise level was unbearable, and twenty-three of us had tossed and turned, covered our heads with pillows, listened to the windows rattle, and done everything we could think of to get to sleep . . . to no avail. By 2:00 AM we were all frustrated and totally frazzled.

Suddenly we hear a shuffling sound coming from the floor

near our director's bed. Generally a sound sleeper herself, this time the nine-decibel snoring was keeping even Charlotte awake, and she had finally decided to do something about it.

"What are you doing?" I whispered.

"I've heard that if you turn on soft music, sometimes it will stop a person's snoring," she said. "So I'm going to plug in the radio and find a quiet station. Maybe it will help."

"You're kidding, right?"

"No. I'm serious."

"Okay. Whatever."

Unfortunately, the radio was halfway down the room from where Charlotte started; so she's crawling along the floor in her pajamas, looking for it. The farther she went, the more

*Eventually, everyone in the room was awake except the two offenders, who started the whole thing. . . .*

women woke up and wanted to know what was going on. Eventually, everyone in the room was awake *except* the two offenders, who started the whole thing, and the entire scenario was starting to become funny. Giggles broke out as Charlotte continued her search—first, for the radio; then, for the electrical outlet to plug it into.

Finally, she found them both, but when she plugged in the radio, it had been left on, and the volume level was extremely loud. The whole room full of women jerked in unison from the sudden blaring music, as Charlotte searched frantically for the volume control and banged her head on the bunk bed under which she had crawled to plug in the radio.

Sudden silence. Two. Three. Four. Then stifled laughter erupted from one end of the dorm room to the other and spread to every corner. Have you ever seen twenty-three women try *not* to laugh? The harder we tried, the funnier the situation became, and the harder we laughed.

Charlotte's now lying on her back on the floor laughing, while at the same time trying to find a quiet music station on the radio. Everyone else is wide awake and in stitches.

At long last, Charlotte found the easy jazz station, turned the volume to low, and made her way back to her bed. The laughter had begun to die down, and everyone was settling back down. The only remaining sound was the radio . . . and our two snoring friends, rattling the rafters; they never heard a thing.

By the way, in case you're wondering, soft music does *not* stop women from snoring. Sigh.

*Mary Hollingsworth*

## IN SEARCH OF *ZZZZZS*

The other night I had a bit of trouble falling asleep. I wasn't at a lecture, studying or watching a rerun of a television talk show; so naturally, I didn't feel the least bit drowsy. I tossed and turned and ended up staring at the ceiling longer than Michelangelo did in the Sistine Chapel.

I tried everything I could to fall asleep.

I drank a glass of warm milk. All that did was give me

an overwhelming desire to sharpen my nails on the carpeting and look under the sofa for mice.

I tried counting sheep, but even they didn't cooperate. Instead of jumping over the fence, they were doing the Hokey Pokey in front of it and I kept losing my count.

Someone once told me that pretending you're being gently rocked to sleep on an ocean liner is a sure cure for insomnia. So I gave this a try. It didn't work either. All I did was worry about how much I should tip the steward.

That's when I decided to watch a little late-night television. After flipping through the dial, I settled on the TV test pattern. It seemed to have the best plot of all the movies on at that time of night.

By 3:00 AM, I was bored with that and still wide awake. I needed something to do. Washing the car would wake up the neighbors, so that was out. I could go grocery shopping, but that didn't sound like much fun. When you're the only one in the store, there's not much point in cart-racing to the sale items.

What I really needed was someone to talk to. Hoping one of the kids might still be awake, I tiptoed down the hall and peeked into their bedrooms. I could hear one of my sons talking in his sleep, so I joined in. Insomniacs do get desperate sometimes.

We had a nice conversation, too, that is, until I asked him about his report card. Then, he suddenly fell into a deep sleep . . . or at least pretended to.

Desperate for more conversation, I tried to think of

someone else who would be up at this hour. Only one answer came to mind—the information operator. I picked up the telephone and dialed. I expected to hear a warm, chipper voice on the other end, but I think I woke her up too. My first clue was when she answered with, "City, please . . . and this had better be important!"

At 4:00 AM, I took my pillow and blanket and tried sleeping on the sofa downstairs. Then, I tried the recliner, and finally, the floor. I watched each second ticking by on the clock. I tried thumbing through a magazine. I did stretching exercises. I took deep breaths. I thought only happy, peaceful thoughts.

I could feel my eyes beginning to get heavy. I yawned a few times. *This is it*, I thought to myself. At last, I was getting sleepy. Rising to my feet, I made my way upstairs to my bedroom. I crawled into bed, laid my head on my pillow, and closed my weary eyes.

Then, the alarm rang.

*Martha Bolton*

**A woman's mind is cleaner than a man's. She changes it more often.**

*Oliver Herford*

### HOW GREAT THOU ART!

When it came time for the offertory, we circulated baskets of apples; instead of collecting money, we hoped to give something to the patients and their families. The whole idea of the service was to be thankful for what we had, as opposed to focusing on what we lost to the illness.

From patient to patient, I carried a huge African basket filled with apples. One very ill woman was furled in a wheelchair, her head slumped on her chest, her hands tightened into the gnarls we associate with the very last days of life. Her caregiver shook her head, indicating that the woman would not be able to hear or understand me, but I wanted the old woman to have an apple. I got down on my knees and tried to make eye contact. It was impossible. I tried to open one of her hands, but it was like a knot.

At that moment the offertory hymn began. The opening bars of "How Great Thou Art" came onto the organ, and my husband, an accomplished baritone, softly began singing the hymn.

The woman uncurled. She straightened up in her wheelchair. At the top of her lungs, she sang every word.

The caregiver gasped. I literally staggered back, then watched as the joy and triumph of the lost self of this woman revealed itself to us. She sang from her heart. As the song ended, she curled back into her chair.

We had reached her.

She had reached us, too, as together we saw for ourselves what we knew to be true: that there, amid what had seemed like darkness, was light we had almost overlooked.

*Jamie Miller*

An archaeologist is the best husband any woman can have: the older she gets, the more interested he is in her.

*Agatha Christie*

"You caught me at a bad time. I'll call you back when my work is done, my house is clean, my husband is happy, my kids are grown, and my thighs are smaller."

## THE SUMMER OF AUNT HATTIE

Our Illinois town was in bad shape in 1980 when my aunt Hattie came to spend the summer with my wife and me. Three years of drought spelled disaster for our farming community. Families had moved away, literally to greener pastures. Dwindling resources and the town's depressed mood had taken a toll on our church too. Members bickered with one another. Some stopped attending services altogether. "God will send us a miracle," our minister promised, but it seemed like a losing battle.

Aunt Hattie's arrival from Florida was a bright spot.

She wore a fancy light blue bonnet when we picked her up at the bus station. "The color goes well with my white hair," she said, and it matched her twinkling eyes. Aunt Hattie had a smile for everyone she met, and never an unkind word. In no time she was "Aunt Hattie" to everyone in town. But she was appalled when we took her with us to church. The organ sat silent while a phonograph played the hymns.

"Mabel Shaw says her arthritis keeps her from playing," I explained.

"She doesn't even come to church anymore," added my wife.

"Why, I love playing the organ," Aunt Hattie said. "I'll fill in, if it's all right."

The congregation was thrilled. Until Sunday rolled around. Aunt Hattie's playing was so off-key it was worse than none at all. After a couple weeks of her at the organ our minister confided that the choir members begged Mabel to come back. "Well," she finally relented, "if you really want me." The following Sunday Mabel took her place at the organ. Aunt Hattie wasn't a bit disappointed. In fact, her blue eyes twinkled while the congregation reveled in Mabel's beautiful playing.

Then one Sunday there were no church bulletins. The minister apologized. Mrs. Jones, who usually did the typing, told him she couldn't spare the time. Most of us knew the reason was the church couldn't afford to pay her. "If anyone here is willing to donate an hour or two," the minister said, "we would surely appreciate it."

Aunt Hattie stood up. "I'll do it," she said.

"Wonderful," exclaimed the minister.

But from the rear of the church I heard someone say, "Oh no!"

Come to find out, poor Aunt Hattie's typing rivaled her organ playing in its ineptitude. Her bulletins had so many words misspelled and run together it was almost impossible to read them. The minister told us privately that an overwhelming number of church people called on Mrs. Jones, pleading with her to take over the typing once more. She had finally agreed to do so.

The next thing Aunt Hattie attempted was the janitorial work. We had no funds for a full-time custodian. Who couldn't handle a broom or a dust cloth? Well, Aunt Hattie, for one. It looked like she swept only where sweeping came easiest. Then she waxed the floor—with such a heavy coating it made walking a hazard! In no time at all Louise Wilson and Margaret Brown volunteered to replace her. We were all amazed. The two ladies hadn't spoken to each other for a year. What on earth had gotten into them?

Aunt Hattie tried her hand at just about everything that summer, with mixed reviews. You couldn't exactly call her a success at any one thing. But you couldn't call her a failure, either. She brought folks back to their jobs and to the church services too.

"We have all learned to love your Aunt Hattie," one lady said to me. It wasn't easy on the ears, or on the eyes, but everyone had to agree that Aunt Hattie had ingratiated herself to them with a willingness to offer herself over to whatever was needed. It would have been perfect, of course, if she had been competent at some of it. But she was an inspiration, nevertheless.

Walking to church on her last Sunday morning with us, my aunt said, "I have a surprise for everyone." My wife looked at her wide-eyed. The church was filled to capacity, both old and new members. The minister sat quietly by the pulpit, admiring his growing congregation. Mabel Shaw rose from the organ and took a seat. Aunt Hattie had warned us that she wanted to make a speech before taking her leave. She walked to the front and faced the congregation.

> Aunt Hattie tried her hand at just about everything that summer, with mixed reviews.

"You have a beautiful church here," she said, "and the members are just as beautiful. I will always remember each and every one of you. Now I would like to play 'In the Garden,' a hymn I love because it makes Jesus seem so close to us."

I never knew our congregation to be so attentive, although I suspected some would have preferred for Aunt Hattie to leave the organ playing to Mabel. I couldn't help thinking this was the kind of patience we'd all been quick to show in the old days, before life had gotten so rough, the drought taking its toll on the land and our good spirit. We all sat silent and peaceful, as if a hard rain had just fallen.

Aunt Hattie walked over to the organ and sat down. She

looked out at us and smiled. I didn't hear a single groan or nervous shuffle. The music soared above us like the song of an angel. The hymn's familiar words flowed through my mind: "He walks with me and He talks with me, and He tells me I am His own. . ." Never had I heard the hymn played so well. What had my aunt been up to? Had she fumbled her organ playing and every job she had undertaken so that we would become a community again? Aunt Hattie would never tell.

When she finished the congregation applauded, and the minister walked over to the pulpit. "There was a time we prayed for a miracle," he said. "God answered our prayers this summer. He sent us Aunt Hattie."

*Marion F. Ash*

Intimacies between women often go backwards, beginning in revelations and ending in small talk.

*Elizabeth Bowen*

## WOMEN WORKING

Men have so much freedom!" I told my friend Bettie, during a discussion about the differences between men and women.

"Like what?" she asked.

"Well, they don't have to wear makeup. Their idea of a bad hair day means it's time for a haircut, and they shop the very day of birthdays and holidays. Getting ready to go somewhere takes me an hour, but my husband jumps in the shower, gets dressed and is dangling the car keys in twenty minutes flat. He doesn't understand why a phone call to check on my mom takes thirty minutes. He makes a five-minute call to his dad and says he's found out everything he needs to know. He also tells me I have a Wal-Mart ministry because women I've never met tell me their life stories in the checkout lines."

"Well, I have to admit," Bettie said, "you don't catch many guys chatting in checkout lines. And, think about it . . . have you ever seen one man at a restaurant table ask another if he'd like to accompany him to the bathroom? We think nothing of it!" "Maybe it's the Venus and Mars thing," I replied. "Have you ever seen a man swoon over anything? Remember the day you found those great shoes on sale and got so excited people swarmed around to check out the bargains? When is the last time you saw a man displaying raw unbridled emotions over a sale? I'd fall over if I ever heard a man say, 'Wow! I'm soooo glad I found this fantastic sale table!'"

"I read somewhere that because men have fewer brain cells than women, they think more analytically with their left brain," Bettie said. "Maybe that's why they carry one hanger bag for a weeklong trip, while we take several suitcases."

"Actually, I think there's really only one thing between men and women I consider unfair treatment," I said seriously. "What's that?" Bettie asked.

"Those road construction signs—the big orange 'Men

Working' ones. Why don't we get to display big orange signs in our driveway while we're cleaning house that say, 'Women Working'?"

"Hey, chalk it up as a *man thing*! They need more recognition," Bettie said jokingly. "Must be those missing brain cells!"

*Susan Duke*

"I typed it that way because I thought punctuation would just slow it down."

My idea of a superwoman is someone who cooks her own meals.

*Mary Hollingsworth*

## THE ONE THAT MATCHES MY HOUSE

After thoroughly examining my old car, my son-in-law, who is a top-notch mechanic, devastated me with the sudden announcement, "You need a new car. Go buy one." I was in my third year of widowhood and felt somewhat like

Alice in Wonderland, having to do all kinds of things that I simply didn't know how to do.

My husband had always bought the cars. I have no interest in automobiles whatsoever. I could never understand why he bought new tires when the old ones still rolled around perfectly. I don't like mechanical things. Instantly a hint of fear began to follow me around. And I had just written a book on how to live fear-free. I also spoke on the subject. Now here I was about to run from the fear of . . . buying a new car.

Some women might have liked that opportunity. Not me! I decided to go into the yard and weed my flower garden.

It was no use. The fear hunched over each flower with me. I had often told people, "When you are afraid of something, do the very thing you fear. Never run from fear."

I stood up and wiped my hands on my slacks, jumped into our old car and headed for the nearest automobile dealership, the one where Jerry had often talked about getting a new car.

I talked to the Lord on the twenty-minute drive: "You know I don't know how to buy a car. I'm doing this because I don't want to battle fear again. I'm not a car person. I don't know anything to ask about or look for in a car. I want to do this quickly and get it over with. I'm starting to be afraid. You promised in Your Word to be a husband to widows. Be one now and show me how to buy the car You want me to have."

As I neared the automobile dealership, a thought came to my mind. It was beige. Just the color beige. And I thought God asked, *What do you know about cars? Let's go with what you know instead of what you don't know.*

I almost laughed. "Lord, I only know the color I'd like. Beige. You know how much I love beige. How good it makes me feel." Many of my clothes are beige, my sheets are beige. I have beige pets, beige stationery. I live in a beige house . . . "Oh, Lord, do you mean I can simply look for a beige car? Could it possibly be that simple? Do You already have my car picked out, knowing how much I love beige?" Such relief and confidence welled up in me that I felt for certain God was answering in the affirmative.

I parked at the dealership and was on my way to the elegant showroom when across the lot, gleaming in the bright sun, I saw the beautiful beige top of a car. *It's yours*, the thought kept running through my mind like an excited child. Once inside the showroom I realized I should probably have changed clothes. But when fear is closing in, there's not always time to dress properly. There was dirt on the knees of my old pants.

An astute young man in his twenties came up. I noticed that all the salesmen wore spiffy blue blazers. "May I help you?" he said and seemed to be overlooking my inappropriate clothing.

"Oh yes. I believe I want that beige car out there." I pointed.

"An excellent selection. Let me explain some of the features. I'd like for you to look under the hood at the fuel injection—"

"Oh no, I don't want to do any of that. All I want to do is take the car home for the weekend." It was late Friday afternoon.

"I beg your pardon?" His flashing smile vanished.

"I have to take it home to see if it matches the paint on my house. If it does . . . it's my car! I believe God has selected that car just for me."

> But when fear is closing in, there's not always time to dress properly.

"God . . . wants you to have that car." He lowered his voice.

"I think so. I need to see if it matches the paint."

"Yes, er . . . well, we don't usually allow people to take cars home for the weekend. Perhaps you'd like to think about it and bring a paint chip on Monday." He had regained composure.

"No. I might be afraid again on Monday. I've never bought a car before. I can do it now. I know I can. Just let me take—"

"Excuse me a moment, please."

He came back with other men dressed in identical blue blazers. They all wore the same smiles. These men were older. One glanced at the dirt on my slacks. "We'd like to assist you in buying a car," he said.

"That's my car out there, the beige one. I know it is. I just need to take it home—"

The young salesman finished the sentence with an I-told-you-so tone of voice: ". . . to see if it matches the paint on her house. She thinks God wants her to have this car."

"Where do you go to church?" the man in charge asked.

"First Baptist, Atlanta."

He looked stunned. "My aunt goes there. It's a good, solid church."

I nodded. They wanted to go out and have me look at the car. When we got close to it, I was surprised at how elegant it was. I would have never, never selected such a car for myself. "This is the top of the line," the young salesman said. "It does have two thousand miles on it. It was a demonstrator. Just came on the lot yesterday. Let's take a drive in it."

It wasn't necessary, but I went with him to be polite.

A short time later I drove the magnificent beige car off the lot for the weekend. Some of the salesmen stood and waved to me. I already knew it was my car and was wonderfully happy that buying a car could be so easy. I still had to go back and do the paperwork, but I felt confident, not at all frightened. I was ecstatic that God had indeed shown me a simple way to buy a car. In the driveway I sat and marveled, my car and the house paint could have come out of the same can! Fear was nowhere around.

I drove back early Monday morning to buy the car. I didn't read the contract, but I did notice that the price was an uneven number. I asked the smiling young salesman to change the number so that the amount would end in zeros. "I hate uneven numbers," I explained. The amount would reduce the price of the car somewhat. But he came back in a few moments with all the numbers in neat zeros except for the first two.

The manager there insisted that I look at some

brochures, and he explained certain features of the car. I smiled, but I wasn't really listening. I was thinking that when the car rolled off the assembly line, God already had selected it for me.

Months later I parked in downtown Atlanta one day. Just as I was getting out of my car, someone parked beside me. To my astonishment it was my car's twin.

The driver of the other car and I looked at each other and smiled. He came over and said, "Well, it certainly seems like you did your homework. I searched for six months, read every consumer report and did a tremendous amount of detailed research to see what new car was the best buy for the money."

I smiled and listened.

"Did you select your car yourself?"

I nodded.

"I'm impressed. I wouldn't think a woman would . . . well, you know, really investigate the automobile industry and come up with such an excellent choice. Congratulations."

"Thank you. The color's nice too, isn't it?"

Walking away from my new car, I realized that a new truth had come with it. When I have to do something hard, something scary, I can zoom in on what I do know about the situation, however insignificant it may seem, and not concentrate on all that I don't know. Then I can call on my Heavenly Father, a God of the nitty-gritty, and He'll help me.

*Marion Bond West*

An optimist is a man who marries his secretary and thinks he'll be able to continue dictating to her.

*Michael Hodgin*


## WORN-OUT WOMAN SYNDROME

You know you're a victim of Worn-Out Woman Syndrome when . . .

You wonder if brewing is really a necessary step for the consumption of coffee.

You ask the drive-through attendant at your favorite Espresso Express if you can get your double mocha to go.

Apart from coffee, tropical-flavored Tums become your sole source of sustenance.

Your family finds you in a fetal position on the kitchen floor after you discovered that the timer on your coffeemaker didn't work.

You keep yelling, "Leave me alone!" even though no one else is anywhere near you.

*Author unknown*


The most pitiful case in psychiatric history concerns the two-faced woman who talked to herself and tried to have the last word.

*Gerald F. Lieberman*

## CUCKOO CLOCK

It's been said that there are three major classifications of inanimate objects: things that break down, things that get lost, and things that no one ever expects to work. I'd like to add a fourth category: things that drive you crazy.

Let me explain. My mom is a big fan of cuckoo clocks. Now, for those of you lucky few who aren't familiar with them, they are an exceptionally expensive and annoying kind of clock, usually birdhouse-shaped with a mechanical bird that pops out of a tiny door and enthusiastically announces "cuckoo" at about eighty-five bazillion decibels every hour, causing you to either jump out of your chair, drop your drink or have a heart attack.

And although it may sound strange, they are very popular and just the sort of thing collectors love. And, hey, I'm sure they are, but frankly, along with porcelain dolls and elephant salt shakers, I just don't see the big draw. (Uh, not that there's anything wrong with either of those things.)

As far as gifts go, my mom isn't an easy person to shop for; so when she asked for a cuckoo clock it all seemed simple enough.

That's when I discovered two important things about cuckoo clocks: (1) quality ones are about the same price as a new sports car, and (2) most of the cuckoo clock shops on this planet are in Germany.

However, I didn't let this bit of knowledge stop me.

Instead, I did what any savvy and sophisticated shopper would do: searched the Internet for a cheap knock-off.

And, lo and behold, I found one. ON SALE. The only drawback was that when it arrived a week later, instead of getting a smallish, quaint clock, I got a hideous looking one about the size of a phone booth. Okay, yes, so maybe I'm exaggerating a bit. But still.

And before you start thinking, *Why didn't you check the size, dummy?* Let me just say, it didn't look like that online. Oh sure, it said something about feet and inches and all that, but who really pays attention to all that stuff anyway?

So I shipped it back and exchanged it for the smaller size, which arrived triumphant on Christmas morning. And I'd like to say I delivered her gift and everyone was happy and that was the end of it. But it wasn't. Little did I know that this only marked the beginning of a long line of cuckoo clocks whizzing back and forth through the United Parcel Service that were, according to my mother, either "too loud," "too soft," "slightly chipped," "unevenly stained" or "didn't sound real enough." Now, the first few problems I can understand, but tell me, how real is a plastic bird coming out of a wooden clock supposed to sound anyway?

The final straw came last week when the UPS delivered to me . . . wait for it . . . the original giant cuckoo clock, which, I might add, I now hate with the passion of a thousand burning suns.

Now it seemed to me I had three choices, none of them

particularly appealing except for the third one which, while emotionally satisfying, was rather violent and financially impractical. So I chose number two, which was to bring it to my mom's apartment who wasn't home, hang it up, and run away. Then contemplate going to live in another country. Preferably one without cuckoo clocks.

And, yes, I admit, this isn't a particularly brilliant or mature plan, but, hey, it was the best I could come up with.

But deep down, I never thought it would really work. So imagine my surprise when my mom called and said, "Thanks for the new clock. It's gorgeous! Say, why didn't you get this kind in the first place?"

Now, there are a lot of things I could've said. But, being a good daughter and a decent sort of person, all that came out was, "You're welcome."

Sometimes it's best that way.

*Debbie Farmer*


The minister was visiting an elderly lady and agreed to pray with her that she might have better health. They knelt together on the floor and he began: "Dear Lord, if it be your will, restore Mrs. McIlroy to her former health."

He felt someone touch him on the arm. "Excuse me," said the old lady, "Call me Lizzie, he won't know me by my married name."

*Phil Mason*

## THE TOP TEN THINGS MEN UNDERSTAND
## ABOUT WOMEN

10.

9.

8.

7.

6.

5.

4.

3.

2.

1.

*Author unknown*

Meeting in the hallway of their home, Jody said to Jeff, "Honey, some people say I'm a really pushy woman. Do you think that's true?"

"Uh, well, let me see . . ."

"Well, make up your mind!" Pushing past him, she said, "And get out of my way!"

*Mary Hollingsworth*

## A KNEADED DIAGNOSES

At a church dinner one night, several women were sitting around the table talking about women's issues—grandkids, menopause and breast cancer.

Nancy said she had discovered her breast cancer in an unusual way. She was lying on her back on the sofa when her cat hopped onto the sofa at her feet and proceeded to walk up Nancy's body. When the cat stepped on Nancy's breast, pain shot through her and she screamed. A visit to the doctor diagnosed her cancer, the treatment for which ultimately saved her life.

"It was a miracle!" said Nancy.

"What miracle?" I asked. "It was just a simple 'cat scan'!"

*Mary Hollingsworth*


First old lady: I hope I look as good as you do when I'm your age.

Second old lady: You did.

*Bob Phillips*


## THE BIG SNORE

The sound actually woke me up. A loud rumble, almost like a foghorn. It stopped abruptly. I drifted back to sleep, but the sound jarred me awake again. "Joe, you hear that?" I asked my husband.

"Yep," he yawned.

"What was it?" I asked.

That's when he rolled over and looked at me, eyes still half shut. "It was you, Mare," he said, "snoring."

Me? "I don't snore!" I insisted. "Women don't snore!"

"Okay," Joe said, rolling over, "but there sure was a lot of noise coming from your side of the bed." I could barely get back to sleep for fear Joe might actually be right. Can it really be true? The idea mortified me.

The next morning I asked Joe if he'd ever heard me snore before. "Oh yeah, it started on our wedding night," he said. I stared at him in shock. We'd been married for thirty-two years. How could I have snored that long and not known it?

"Has it always been this bad?"

"It used to be soft, like a purring cat, but lately it's more like a freight train. You've definitely gotten worse," Joe said.

"That's terrible!" Then I thought of something really terrible. I'd signed up for a trip to Europe with a group from the college where I taught, and my friend Shelley was going to be my roommate. Now, it was one thing to snore with Joe. But what if I kept Shelley up at night? How embarrassing. "What can I do?" I asked Joe.

"Go see Dr. Sam. Maybe he can help you." Then he added with an exaggerated yawn, "And me."

*You see the doctor when you're sick, not when you're snoring like a walrus*, I fretted. But I kept thinking of Shelley and the trip and this racket I was apparently making. Maybe there was a medical reason. I made an appointment with the doctor.

"So, you have a snoring problem," Dr. Sam practically shouted as he led me to the exam room. "*Shhh!*" I said, putting my hand up like a traffic cop. Everyone in the waiting room would hear. Dr. Sam ignored my protests and started asking a barrage of questions. Recent weight gain? I cringed. Well, maybe a few pounds over the holidays . . . Allergies? No, unless you count those sneezing fits I've been having every morning lately. Family history of snoring? Mom never snored, but Dad could rock the house.

> You see the doctor when you're sick, not when you're snoring like a walrus, I fretted.

Dr. Sam leveled with me. "Marilyn, I'm glad you told me about your snoring. Lots of women are too self-conscious to talk about it. But snoring can be a sign of a more serious problem."

"I already have a serious problem," I said. "I'm taking a trip to Europe and I'm sharing a room with another woman. I'll die if I keep her awake."

"Well, then, Marilyn, let's get to the bottom of this," he said. Dr. Sam sent me to a sleep disorders clinic—where I had to sleep in front of a group of complete strangers who monitored my every breath . . . and snore.

"Don't worry, we've heard much worse," one of the technicians told me afterward. I suppose he meant it to be reassuring. Next was the allergist who put me through a battery of tests and evaluated my breathing functions.

Finally the verdict came. I didn't have a serious disorder but I did have a deviated septum and a weak soft palate. Throw my allergies into the mix and I'd gone from a purring cat into a rhinoceros. "I can give you something for your allergies," Dr. Sam said, "but what you really need is surgery."

Surgery! There wasn't any time! The trip was coming up. "Is there anything else I can do right now?" I asked.

"Tell your roommate," he said. "I'm sure she'll understand."

Right. I'd just call Shelley up and say, "Oh, by the way, Joe says I snore like a freight train so don't plan on getting a lot of sleep in Europe." I'll tell my prayer group, I decided. We talked about everything. They would understand. They'd help me. But instead of sympathy I heard a string of snoring horror stories.

"I once roomed with a woman who snored," one woman remarked. "She sounded like a lawnmower! There was nothing to be done. I had to move." Another woman chimed in. "I can't imagine anything more humiliating!" They got so caught up in sharing their own horror stories that they almost forgot to pray for me!

The day before the trip, my suitcase was packed, my passport and tickets put where I wouldn't forget them. But I was far from ready. I paced in our bedroom, wondering what I should do. Joe tried to tell me I was making too big a deal out of this, but I wasn't having it. Besides, he was probably looking forward to finally getting a good night's sleep. *Lord*, I said, *why did you make me a snorer? How could you?*

And then it hit me. I had been praying to God to help me stop snoring, but despite all I tried, I never trusted God that even if I snored, he could make things right. Now I was desperate. *Okay, Lord, I'm turning this one over to you. Snoring or no snoring, I'm trusting that everything will be okay. Amen.*

The next day I arrived at the airport early, looking all over for Shelley. I wanted to warn her before we both got on that plane. I finally saw her at the gate. I took a deep breath and said, "Shelley, I have something really important to tell you before we go. I snore. Joe can hardly sleep. I'm so sorry to tell you now. Maybe we can switch roommates if we need to . . ."

"Marilyn," Shelley interrupted, "I have something to tell you. I've been having sinus problems. I snore too. But I've got the perfect solution for us." She reached into her bag. "Here," she said. She handed me a pair of bright orange industrial-strength earplugs. We both burst out laughing.

Mid-flight I peeked through the window at the sun rising over the Atlantic. I basked in a feeling of relief. No, not relief, really. Gratitude. Gratitude that there was nothing more wrong with me than something a simple surgical procedure would remedy (and a pair of earplugs). Gratitude that Shelley was a good-natured and understanding friend. And grateful above everything that God loves me, snores and all.

*Marilyn Strube*

A woman needs four men in her life: a banker, an actor, a minister and a mortician. One for the money, two for the show, three to get ready and four to go!

*Michael Hodgin*

How can you tell which bottle contains the PMS medicine? It's the one with bite marks on the cap.

*Author unknown*

### JUMPIN' JILL

While our choir was on tour in Scotland several years ago, our dear Scottish friend, Jill Noer, acted as guide and host for us. Jill was a jolly soul, who loved to laugh and sing. We loved her, and she loved us. It was a match made in heaven.

Because we had a relatively small group traveling on this particular trip, instead of hiring a huge tour bus with a professional driver and guide, we rented two smaller vans. And another Scottish friend, Bob Halliday, drove his car. So we had a three-vehicle convoy wherever we went . . . and we went a lot!

Now, there are two things you need to know about Americans traveling in Scottish vans. First of all, Scottish vans are not nearly as large as American vans. And the seats are not nearly as wide as seats in American vans (I wonder what that means?). Therefore, as the third person in a three-seat section, I found myself the odd-one-out on this trip, and my posterior was half on and half off the seat most of the time. I spent the entire trip perched precariously on the edge of the seat and on a suitcase in the aisle. (Oh, how I wished for my comfy recliner at home!)

Second, the roads in Scotland are, for the most part, small two-lane roads with no shoulders that meander in and out of the steep, heather-covered, rocky hills, around lakes and through tiny villages. Again, not like most American roads. Even on a good day, it takes concentration and care to maneuver them.

Add to that the fact that we had two American drivers, who are used to driving in the right-hand lane, now navigating these tricky roads in the left-hand lane, and you had a perfect recipe for disaster in the making.

One of those drivers was our fearless director and my best friend, Charlotte Greeson, whom I refer to as "Mario" (for Andretti), because she often feels "the need for speed." A dyed-in-the-wool sports car enthusiast, for thirty years Charlotte drove nothing but a Nissan 300ZX. So the fact that she was driving a van that had very little pick up or speed was, to say the least, frustrating to her. However, for the most part, she took it good naturedly and just pedaled as fast as she could to keep up with the other van.

Because Jill loved Charlotte, she chose to ride shotgun in the van Charlotte was driving . . . at least at the beginning. So these two delightful women are side by side in the front of the van, I'm in the middle hanging on (literally) for dear life, and the van is struggling up the hills with its more-than-full load of Americans, luggage, sound equipment, and other necessities of a performing troupe.

Did I mention that it was foggy that day? Oh, sorry. A small detail I overlooked. Boy, was it foggy that day! We could barely see the back of the van in front of us. And we were headed into the highlands for a concert at a cathedral in an outlying area.

It might have been a good idea to cancel the concert, but when you've traveled from the US to Scotland to sing, you don't just cancel. "The show must go on!" So off we went into the foggy morning to keep our engagement.

The farther we went into the highlands, the more our van struggled to get up the hills. Each hill was higher than the last one, because we were steadily climbing to the top of a mountain. When we topped a hill, Charlotte would give it all the gas she could down the other side, trying to pick up enough speed to get up the next hill. And by the top of that next hill, Old Blue was choking for air and sputtering for all it was worth.

Meanwhile, Jill is getting nervous at Charlotte's erratic driving. She's begun to hang on to the dashboard and the door rest in white-knuckle fashion as Mario is urging Old Blue along with all her might. In fact, Jill wasn't alone. The rest of us in the van were getting a little edgy too; so we began to make wise cracks and jokes to cover up our nervousness.

Jill, on the other hand, has begun making comments, like, "You know, Charlotte, I'll bet we could call the cathedral and they would let us reschedule the concert to another day." Or, "Charlotte, are you sure this is a good idea?" Or, "Say, would you like for me to drive for a while? You must be tired."

To which Charlotte replied, "Jill, darlin', if I stop this van now, we'll never get up enough speed to get to the top of this mountain." And she just kept driving like a mad woman.

Suddenly, at the top of a hill, we could see there was just one more major hill and we would be at the top of the mountain. Unfortunately, it was an extremely long, steep hill, and Charlotte knew there was no way Old Blue was going to make it to the top. So, making a quick decision, she gunned Old Blue and took off down the hill at lightning speed.

> Each hill was higher than the last one, because we were steadily climbing to the top of a mountain.

"Hang on, everybody!" she said, as she whipped into the oncoming traffic lane to go around the other van. Of course, it was so foggy she couldn't see if anything was coming or not; she was just going for broke.

"Oh, dear Lord!" screamed Jill, as she hid her face in her hands.

"Wahoo! Wahoo! Wahoo!" yelled someone from the back of the van.

And you should have seen the shocked expression on the face of the driver of the first van as we went flying past them in the fog. It was a Kodak moment!

Meanwhile, I'm doing a balancing act on my half-seat,

half-suitcase perch, praying like there's no tomorrow, and wondering if we're headed for a *Thelma and Louise* moment off the side of a Scottish mountain with Mario at the wheel.

Somehow, though, with Charlotte's coaxing, Old Blue coughed and choked to the top of the mountain in the middle of nowhere and finally coasted to a trembling stop in front of . . . you won't believe this . . . McDonald's!

We hadn't come to a complete stop when Jill almost ripped the door off its hinges and jumped out of the van with a wild-eyed expression, saying, "Oh, dear Lord! Oh, dear Lord!"

The rest of us took a deep breath, looked out the window to see McDonald's and collapsed in hysterics at the irony of it all. What a morning!

In case you're wondering, we made it to our concert on time . . . but Jill rode the rest of the way with Bob in his car. Wimp!

*Mary Hollingsworth*

"What are you worried about? I was a cheerleader . . .
Everyone will remember what I looked like."

Woman (on the phone): Doctor, come quick! Little Omar just swallowed my fountain pen!

Doctor: I'll be right there. What are you doing in the meantime?

Woman: I'm using a ballpoint.

*Anne Kostick*

## AND GOD MADE WOMAN . . .

By the time the Lord made woman, he was into his sixth day of working overtime. An angel appeared and said, "Why are you spending so much time on this one?"

And the Lord answered and said, "Have you seen the spec sheet on her? She has to be completely washable, but not plastic, have two hundred movable parts, all replaceable, run on black coffee and leftovers, have a lap that can hold three children at one time, have a kiss that can cure anything from a scraped knee to a broken heart, and have six pairs of hands."

The angel tried to stop the Lord. "This is too much work for one day. Wait until tomorrow to finish."

"But I can't!" the Lord protested. I am so close to finishing this creation that is so close to my own heart. She already heals herself when she is sick *and* can work eighteen-hour days."

The angel moved closer and touched the woman. "But you have made her so soft, Lord."

"She is soft," the Lord agreed, "but I have also made her tough. You have no idea what she can endure or accomplish."

"Will she be able to think?" asked the angel. The Lord replied, "Not only will she be able to think, she will be able to reason, and negotiate."

The angel then noticed something and reached out and touched the woman's cheek.

"Oops, it looks like you have a leak with this model. I told you that you were trying to put too much into this one."

"That's not a leak," the Lord objected, "that's a tear!"

"What's the tear for?" the angel asked.

The Lord said, "The tear is her way of expressing her joy, her sorrow, her pain, her disappointment, her loneliness, her grief, and her pride."

The angel was impressed. "You are a genius, Lord. You thought of everything, for women are truly amazing."

*Kilie John and Alie Stibbe*

"For God so loved the world that He gave His only begotten Son, that whosoever believeth in Him should not perish, but have ever-laughing life."

*A Five-Year-Old's Version of John 3:16*

# Credits

**CHAPTER ONE—YOU'VE GOTTA BE KIDDING!**

Babb, Martin. *When did Caesar Become a Salad and Jeremiah a Bullfrog?* West Monroe, LA: Howard, 2005.

Bolton, Martha. *Honey, The Carpet Needs Weeding Again.* Ann Arbor, MI: Servant, 1993.

Bonham, Tal D. *The Treasury of Clean Jokes.* Nashville, TN: Broadman & Holman, 1997.

Brock, Anita. "The Great Boating Excursion." Used by permission.

Brunsting, Bernard. *Light Up Your Life with a Laugh.* © 1993. Used by permission.

——. *The Ultimate Guide to Good Clean Humor.* Uhrichsville, OH: Barbour, 2000. Used by permission.

Callaway, Phil. *Who Put a Skunk in the Trunk?* Sisters, OR: Multnomah, 1999, 2005. Used by permission of Multnomah Publishers Inc.

Clairmont, Patsy. *Normal is Just a Setting on Your Dryer*, a Focus on the Family book published by Tyndale House Publishers. Copyright © 1993. All rights reserved. International copyright secured. Used by permission.

Faulkner, Paul. *Making Things Right When Things Go Wrong.* West Monroe, LA: Howard, 1996.

Ford, Joe Taylor. *The Executive Speech Newsletter.* St. Johnsbury, VT: Words Ink, 1990.

Hall, Doug. *Reborn to Be Wild!* Madison, WI: InterVarsity, 1993.

Hodgen, Michael. *1001 Humorous Illustrations for Public Speaking*. Copyright © 1994 by Michael Hodgin. Used by permission of the Zondervan Corporation.

Jantz, Stan and Bruce Bickel. *Laughables*. Eugene, OR: Harvest House, 1984. Used by permission of authors.

Linamen, Karen Scalf. *Welcome to the Funny Farm: The All-True Misadventures of a Woman on the Edge*. Grand Rapids, MI: Fleming H. Revell, a division of Baker Publishing Group, 2001.

Nelson, Lee. "I'll Be Seeing You." Used by permission.

Phillips, Bob. *The Best of the Good Clean Jokes*. Eugene, OR: Harvest House, 2001. Used by permission. www.harvesthousepublishers.com.

———. *Bob Phillips' Encyclopedia of Good Clean Jokes*. Eugene, OR: Harvest House, 2001. Used by permission. www.harvesthousepublishers.com.

Phillips, Marvin. *Never Lick a Frozen Flagpole*. West Monroe, LA: Howard, 1999.

Stibbe, Alie and Killy John. *Bursting at the Seams*. Oxford, UK: Monarch, 2004.

Stibbe, Mark and J. John. *A Box of Delights*. Oxford, UK: Monarch, 2001.

———. *A Bucket of Surprises*. Oxford, UK: Monarch, 2002.

### CHAPTER TWO—A VIEW FROM THE PEW

*The World's Greatest Collection of Church Jokes*, published by Barbour Publishing, Inc. Uhrichsville, OH: Barbour, 2000. Used by permission.

Bolton, Martha. *Honey, The Carpet Needs Weeding Again*. Ann Arbor, MI: Servant, 1993.

Braude, Jacob M. *Braude's Treasury of Wit and Humor for All Occasions*. Paramus, NJ: Prentice Hall, 1991.

Gonsalves, Sean. "An Easter Story." *Cape Cod Times, Universal Press Syndicate*.

Hafer, Dick. *Dick Hafer's Church Chuckles*. Green Forest, AR: New Leaf Press, 1995. Used by permission.

Lowry, Mark. *Out of Control*. Nashville, TN: W Publishing, 1996. Reprinted by permission. All rights reserved.

The late Dr. Bruce McIver, *Stories I Couldn't Tell While I was a Pastor*. Dallas, TX: Word, 1991. Used by permission.

Pelton, Robert W. *Partnership*. Mt. Juliet, TN: January–February 1987.

Phelps, Steve. *All God's Children Got Gum in Their Hair*. Madison, WI: Intervarsity Press, 1994. Copyright © Steve Phelps. Used with permission.

Phillips, Bob. *The World's Greatest Collection of Clean Jokes*. Eugene, OR: Harvest House, 1998. Used by permission. www.harvesthousepublishers.com.

Portlock, Rob. *Way Off the Church Wall*. Madison, WI: Intervarsity Press, 1989. Copyright © Rob Portlock. Used by permission.

Stibbe, Mark and J. John. *A Box of Delights*. Oxford, UK: Monarch, 2001.

Streiker, Lowell D. *Nelson's Big Book of Laughter*. Nashville, TN: Thomas Nelson, 2000. Used by permission of Thomas Nelson, Inc.

## CHAPTER THREE—PARENTS WANTED!

Bonham, Tal D. *The Treasury of Clean Jokes*. Nashville: Broadman & Holman, 1997. Used by permission.

Chambers, Mary. *Motherhood is Stranger Than Fiction*. Downers Grove, IL: InterVarsity Press, 1990. Used by permission of InterVarsity Press, PO Box 1400, Downers Grove, IL 60515. www.ivpress.com.

Clairmont, Patsy. *God Uses Cracked Pots*, a Focus on the Family book published by Tyndale House Publishers. Copyright © 1999. All rights reserved. International copyright secured. Used by permission.

Davis, Melodie M. *Why Didn't I Just Raise Radishes?*, pp. 96–97. Copyright © 1994 by Herald Press, Scottsdale, PA 15683. Used by permission.

Fabry, Chris. Reprinted from *At the Corner of Mundane and Grace*. Copyright © 1999 by Chris Fabry. Used by permission of WaterBrook Press, Colorado Springs, CO. All rights reserved.

Freeman, Becky. *Peanut Butter Kisses and Mud Pie Hugs.* Copyright © 2000 by Becky Freeman. Published by Harvest House Publishers, Eugene, OR. Used by permission. www.harvesthousepublishers.com.

Graham, Vicki. "Poking and Persistence." Used by permission.

Hahn, Jennifer. *The Teacher, Teacher Joke Book.* Published by Barbour Publishing, Inc. Uhrichsville, OH: Barbour, 2004. Used by permission.

Hollingsworth, Mary. "Without Children." Administered by Shady Oaks Studio, 1507 Shirley Way, Bedford, TX 76022. Used by permission.

Kennedy, Nancy. *Mom on the Run.* Sisters, OR: Multnomah, 1996. Used by permission.

———. *Prayers God Always Answers.* Colorado Springs: WaterBrook, 1999.

Myers, James. *A Treasury of Religious Humor.* South Bend, IN: And Books, 1994. Used by permission.

Peel, Kathy. *Stomach Virus and Other Forms of Family Bonding.* Nashville: W Publishing, a division of Thomas Nelson, Inc., 1993. All rights reserved.

Phillips, Bob. *The Best of the Good Clean Jokes.* Eugene, OR: Harvest House, Copyright © 2001. Used by permission. www.harvesthousepublishers.com.

Stibbe, Mark and J. John. *A Barrel of Fun.* Oxford, UK: Monarch, 2003.

Toler, Stan. *The Buzzards Are Circling But God's Not Finished with Me Yet.* Colorado Springs: River Oak, a division of Cook Communications Ministries, 2001. Used with permission. May not be further reproduced. All rights reserved.

#### CHAPTER FOUR—MEDICAL MAYHEM

Bessie and Beulah. Quote used by permission. For more information visit www.brataproductions.com.

Buchwald, Art. "The Miracle Drugs Abroad" from *Don't Forget to Write.* © 1960 by Art Buchwald. London, UK: Gollancz, a division of Orion Publishing.

Johnson, Derric. *Lists The Book, Vol. II.* Orlando: Y.E.S.S. Press, 1995. Used by permission.

Lowry, Mark. *Out of Control*. Nashville, TN: W Publishing, a division of Thomas Nelson, Inc., 1996. Reprinted by permission. All rights reserved.

The late Dr. Bruce McIver, *Stories I Couldn't Tell While I was a Pastor*. Dallas, TX: Word, 1991. Used by permission.

Myers, James. *A Treasury of Medical Humor*. South Bend, IN: And Books, 1993. Used by permission.

Phillips, Bob. *The World's Greatest Collection of Clean Jokes*. Eugene, OR: Harvest House, 1998. Used by permission. www.harvesthousepublishers.com.

———. *Over the Hill and On a Roll*. Eugene, OR: Harvest House, 1998. Used by permission. www.harvesthousepublishers.com.

Stibbe, Alie and Killy John. *Bursting at the Seams*. Oxford, UK: Monarch, 2004.

Swindoll, Luci. *Wide My World, Narrow My Bed*. Nashville: Thomas Nelson, 1982.

Streiker, Lowell D. *Nelson's Big Book of Laughter*. Nashville, TN: Thomas Nelson, 2000. Used by permission of Thomas Nelson, Inc.

Whaley, Bo. *The Official Redneck Handbook*. Nashville, TN: Thomas Nelson, 1987. Used by permission of Thomas Nelson, Inc.

## CHAPTER FIVE—MAIN STREET MIRTH

Bonham, Tal D. *The Treasury of Clean Jokes*. Nashville, TN: Broadman & Holman, 1997.

Freeman, Becky. *Lemonade Laughter and Laid-Back Joy*. Eugene, OR: Harvest House, 2001. Used by permission. www.harvesthousepublishers.com.

Green, Michael. *Illustrations for Biblical Preaching*. Grand Rapids, MI: Baker, 1989.

Grizzard, Lewis. *Chili Dawgs Always Bark at Night*. New York: Random House, 1965. Copyright © Lewis Grizzard. Used by permission. www.lewisgrizzard.com.

Hollingsworth, Mary. "You Can't Do That." Administered by Shady Oaks Studio, 1507 Shirley Way, Bedford, TX 76022. Used by permission.

Kraus, James. *Bloopers, Blunders, Quips, Jokes, and Quotes.* Wheaton, IL: Tyndale House, 2005. Used by permission.

Myers, James. *A Treasury of Medical Humor.* South Bend, IN: And Books, 1993. Used by permission.

Phillips, Bob. *The Ultimate Joke Book.* Eugene, OR: Harvest House, 2002. Used by permission. www.harvesthousepublishers.com.

Streiker, Lowell D. *Nelson's Big Book of Laughter.* Nashville, TN: Thomas Nelson, 2000. Used by permission of Thomas Nelson, Inc.

*World's Best Bathroom Book.* ©2000. Used with permission by Cook Communications Ministries. All rights reserved. www.cookministries.com.

Wright, Rusty and Linda Raney. *500 Clean Jokes and Humorous Stories* published by Barbour Publishing, Inc. Uhrichsville, OH: Barbour, 1985. Used by permission.

### CHAPTER SIX—SMILES OVER COFFEE

Bolton, Martha. *Never Ask Delilah for a Trim.* Grand Rapids, MI: Bethany House, a division of Baker Book House, 1998.

Eller, Suzanne T. "That's What Friends Do." Used by permission. tseller@daretobelieve.org.

Greeson, Charlotte. "The Nineteen and Half Finger Duet." Used by permission.

Hollingsworth, Mary. Administered by Shady Oaks Studio, 1507 Shirley Way, Bedford, TX 76022. Used by permission.

Johnson, Barbara. *Fresh Elastic for Stretched out Moms.* Grand Rapids, MI: Baker Book House, 2003.

Linamen, Karen Scalf. *Just Hand Over the Chocolate and No One Will Get Hurt.* Grand Rapids: Fleming H. Revell, a division of Baker Publishing Group, 1999.

Phillips, Bob. *The World's Greatest Collection of Clean Jokes.* Eugene, OR: Harvest House, 1998. Used by permission. www.harvesthousepublishers.com.

## CHAPTER SEVEN—JUST CALL THEM LAUGH LINES!

Babb, Martin. *When did Caesar Become a Salad and Jeremiah a Bullfrog?* West Monroe, LA: Howard, 2005

Bolton, Martha. *I Think, Therefore I Have a Headache.* Grand Rapids, MI: Bethany House, a division of Baker Publishing Group, 2003.

Brunsting, Bernard. *Light Up Your Life with a Laugh.* © 1993. Used by permission.

Chambers, Mary. *Church is Stranger Than Fiction.* Downers Grove, IL: InterVarsity Press, 1990. Used by permission of InterVarsity Press, PO Box 1400, Downers Grove, IL 60515. www.ivpress.com.

English, Roy. Originally published in *When I Am an Old Coot* (Salt Lake City: Gibbs Smith, Publisher, 1995). Used with permission.

Hodgin, Michael. *1001 Humorous Illustrations for Public Speaking.* Copyright © 1994 by Michael Hodgin. Used by permission of the Zondervan Corporation.

Hollingsworth, Mary. Administered by Shady Oaks Studio, 1507 Shirley Way, Bedford, TX 76022. Used by permission.

Kennedy, Nancy. *Mom on the Run.* Sisters, OR: Multnomah, 1996. Used by permission.

Loveless, Caron Chandler. *Honey, They Shrunk My Hormones.* West Monroe, LA: Howard, 2003.

Lowry, Mark. *Out of Control.* Nashville, TN: W Publishing, 1996. Reprinted by permission. All rights reserved.

Macias, Kathi. *Confessions from the Far Side of Thirty.* Colorado Springs, CO: Cook Communications, 1993. www.kathimacias.com.

Mullen, Tom. *Middle Age & Other Mixed Blessings.* Grand Rapids, MI: Fleming H. Revell, a division of Baker Book House, 1991.

Phillips, Marvin. *Never Lick a Frozen Flagpole.* West Monroe, LA: Howard, 1999.

Sanders, Al. *I'm Trying to Number My Days*. Colorado Springs: WaterBrook, 1998.

Streiker, Lowell D. *Nelson's Big Book of Laughter*. Nashville, TN: Thomas Nelson, 2000. Used by permission of Thomas Nelson, Inc.

Stibbe, Mark and J. John. *A Box of Delights*. Oxford, UK: Monarch, 2001.

Toler, Stan. "The Spirit is Willing But the Dentures are Missing." Used by permission.

## CHAPTER EIGHT—LIPSTICK LAMPOON

Bolton, Martha. *Never Ask Delilah for a Trim*. Grand Rapids, MI: Bethany House, a division of Baker Book House, 1998.

Bottom, Renae. "Chronic Purse-Stuffers Club." This article originally appeared in *Marriage Partnership*. Copyright © fall 1997. Reprinted by permission. www.marriagepartnership.com.

Cohl, Aaron H. ed., *The Friars Club Encyclopedia of Jokes*. New York: Black Dog & Leventhal, 1997.

Duke, Susan. *God Things Come in Small Packages*. Lancaster, PA: Starburst, 2000. Used by permission. suzieduke@juno.com; www.suzieduke.com.

Farmer, Debbie. "Cuckoo Clock." debbie.farmer@yahoo.com or visit www.familydaze.com

Hodgin, Michael. *1001 Humorous Illustrations for Public Speaking*. Copyright © 1994 by Michael Hodgin. Used by permission of the Zondervan Corporation.

Hollingsworth, Mary. Administered by Shady Oaks Studio, 1507 Shirley Way, Bedford, TX 76022. Used by permission. All rights reserved.

Kostick, Anne. *3650 Jokes, Puns, & Riddles*. (New York: Workman, 1998).

Kraus, James. *Bloopers, Blunders, Quips, Jokes, and Quotes*. Wheaton, IL: Tyndale House, 2005. Used by permission.

Miller, Jamie C. *Mother's Miracles*. New York: William Morrow, 1999.